ALL ABOUT
CELEBRATION

NURSERY WORLD

TES
THE TIMES EDUCATIONAL SUPPLEMENT

NURSERY WORLD

TES
THE TIMES EDUCATIONAL SUPPLEMENT

Editor Edward FitzGerald
Art Editor Nicola Liddiard

Managing Editor Patricia Grogan
Consultant Marian Whitehead

Photography Andy Crawford

First published in Great Britain in 1999 by
Times Supplements Limited
Admiral House, 66–68 East Smithfield, London E1 9XY

A CIP catalogue record for this book is available
from the British Library

ISBN 1-84122-008-6

Colour reproduction by Prima Creative Services, UK
Printed and bound in Belgium by Proost

Nursery World would like to thank the children
and staff at the following Teddies nurseries
for taking part in this book:
Teddies Nursery, Chiswick, London
Teddies Nursery, Northwood, Middlesex

CONTENTS

INTRODUCTION

All About Celebration contains over 100 activities in five chapters and a sixth chapter with useful reference material. Chapter one helps you prepare for the subsequent chapters, each of which explores one avenue of the book's central theme. The activities are self-contained, but also build on from each other, so you can dip into several chapters when planning your theme, or use complete chapters. All the activities are underpinned by seven areas of learning. The topic web on pages 10–11 shows you into which areas each activity falls and each activity has symbols representing those areas of learning covered.

Planning a curriculum

The activities in this book are suitable for curriculum planning following all the early-years guidelines across the United Kingdom. It is widely accepted that young children learn most effectively through first-hand experiences presented through investigative, sensory, imaginative, creative and constructive, play-based activities. Children should be given opportunities to observe, represent, recall, describe, and question. This book gives many ideas for developing these skills, although it should not be seen as providing a complete curriculum. The book's main purpose is to help you build a balanced, varied and interesting curriculum for children of nursery age when presenting aspects of the complex theme of Celebration. Each activity covers one or more of the following areas of learning: Personal, Social and Emotional Development, Language and Literacy, Mathematics, Science and Technology, Time and Place, Physical Development and Creative Development.

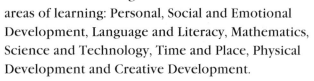

Personal, Social and Emotional Development

This area of development is a crucial aspect of the early-years curriculum, and as such should be given special attention in all settings. Young children need to develop self-confidence and a sense that they are valued and respected. This helps them to approach and communicate with others, both adults and children, and to be able to take responsibility for their own actions. Through communicating with others, children begin to build friendships outside their family and learn the importance of co-operation, sharing and taking turns. The activities in this book help develop these social skills, so it is important that you allow children to do as much on their own as possible, only intervening when they become frustrated or bored with a project.

The activities encourage children to talk about their lives and families, discuss their feelings and make their own decisions. This book will help children to respect both their own cultures and traditions and a range of other cultures, races and religions.

Language and Literacy

Through talking and listening, children begin to develop their language and literacy skills which are crucial for the development of all other areas of learning. As children carry out the activities in this book, encourage them to talk about what they are doing, and always praise them verbally for their efforts. Make sure you stress the importance of listening to any instructions given. Many of the activities focus on important stories from diverse cultures and can encourage children to report on events in their lives, describe objects by texture, colour, shape and size, and make up their own stories . Try to introduce as many different forms of language as possible, including rhymes and songs, and give the children the opportunity to use these forms themselves.

It is vital that your book corner or reading area is comfortable and inviting for the children so that they are encouraged to use it, even when not specifically directed by an adult. The shelves should be stocked with a wide range of titles, including fiction, reference, poetry and rhyme. When reading to the children, try to use books that have a lot of colour illustrations; relevant pictures help children to grasp the meaning of the text.

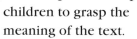

Many activities demonstrate the different purposes of writing and encourage children to produce their own emergent writing as a result of what they have learned. This could be in writing invitations, where you should be on hand to act as a scribe to help children communicate their meaning, playing independently or putting together a class book with other children.

Mathematics

This book will give children a strong sense of number, shape and space through enjoyable and attractive play-based activities. As with the other areas of learning, mathematical development can be approached through many different activities, so it is important to direct learning to that aim where appropriate. Children have the chance to sort and classify items, for example, when tidying up props after a role-play activity. Furthermore, in the step-by-step cooking activities, children will be able to count out items and begin to understand units of weight and measurement in order to complete the recipes correctly.

It is important that children hear you using relevant mathematical language in the setting. There is the opportunity to use comparative language, such as bigger/smaller, and children can improve their counting skills by singing number rhymes. Whatever you do, it is essential that you tailor activities to suit children at all levels of proficiency, from those barely able to count, to those who use numbers over ten with confidence.

Science and Technology

Science, by its very nature, permeates everything in the world around us, thus offering opportunities for investigation in all the activities featured in this book. Learning in the early years should encourage children's curiosity and wonder about the world around them and instil in them a positive attitude towards enquiry and investigation. Children should ask questions about why and how things happen. They can be helped to use the activities, and the information provided by adults, in order to find answers to their own questions. In this way they will be able to make sense of their experiences of the world, starting with first-hand experiences and eventually moving on to tackle more abstract and complex ideas

The term technology, when used in an early-years context, covers all aspects of model-making and the use of technological equipment. Children should have the opportunity to explore a range of tools and materials to develop their construction skills. They should learn to examine what they have made and find ways that it can be improved to perform its function properly. As they develop, children start to choose the best materials for a particular task. In all the learning in this area, it is vital that early-years professionals ask careful, open-ended questions to encourage children to think about, question and describe what they are doing.

Time and Place

This area of learning is concerned with where people live, their relationships with each other and the environment, both in the past and the present. All the celebrations in this book find their roots somewhere in history, so children have the opportunity to learn about and use language relevant to events in the past. They can place themselves in the past and draw on first-hand experiences to share events and celebrations that they have experienced with their families, adding to their growing vocabulary about time, place and story-telling.

With festivals and celebrations drawn from all over the globe, the activities lead children to a greater awareness of the world, both geographically and culturally. Closer to home, visits to places outside the setting will furnish children with a greater understanding of their immediate environment and its inherent cultural diversity. They will develop a concern for this environment and begin to learn how and in what ways it is affected by people. By visiting a range of different places, children develop a sense of place and begin to understand the work of people who live locally. Do not forget that many of the books you read to the children will contain valuable information for developing the themes of time and place.

Physical Development

This area of learning is concerned with the development of children's gross and fine motor skills and their physical well-being. Activities that encourage children to run, jump and dance help to promote good health and build confidence, control, co-ordination and strength. At the same time physical activities heighten children's awareness of the space around them and develop their personal and social skills as they work and play alongside their peers.

By introducing children to activities that include threading, painting and using tools such as scissors, you are encouraging them to develop their fine motor skills. Learning how to hold and control a range of tools and instruments will also help children to develop writing skills. Young children are naturally very active and inquisitive, using their physical skills to explore their immediate environment, so it is important that you use the activities in this book to encourage them to develop these skills. There should be a wide range of tools and materials available to use at all times if children are to achieve these aims.

Creative Development

Here, children are encouraged to express themselves and explore feelings and ideas through a wide range of media, such as art, music and role play. It is important that your art area is equipped with materials suitable for both two- and three-dimensional work. Ensure that the area is suitable for children to experiment with colour, shape and form, both during and outside directed play.

This book gives suggestions on how you can incorporate both music and dance into the curriculum. Ideas are given for how to make instruments in the setting and for how you might include dances relevant to particular festivals. There is also the opportunity for children to listen and respond to songs.

Using role play is an excellent way to motivate children to communicate their own ideas and feelings, to understand the lives and feelings of others and to co-operate with them. Also, by using a range of props and resources, children are stimulated to use their imagination in a creative way. In general, you should encourage children to be imaginative and creative in the ways they find to express their understanding of the world around them.

Assessing children's learning

There should be an ongoing programme of assessment in your setting, designed to inform staff, parents and carers of where children stand with regard to their learning. You should have clear aims for what you hope to achieve before you start so that you can focus your assessment on particular areas. Each activity in this book has more than one area of learning, expressed as a learning outcome. To make your assessment manageable, choose no more than two of these to approach at a time . When planning which activities and what learning you hope to achieve over the week, allow time in your schedule for assessment. Always keep a notebook handy so that you can record any significant events relevant to children's learning. Listen attentively to how they respond to open questions, focus on how they interact with other children and adults and pay close attention to how they work with materials, looking at what they choose to make. Draw up a checklist of expected learning outcomes from the activities you plan to assess, leaving enough space to make comments alongside. Make use of parents' and carers' knowledge of their children to add useful information to your records. The results will indicate each child's strengths and inform you of any particular needs the child may have. You can use this information to help plan future activities. It is important that you are sensitive to what the child has learned, even if it is not what you expected.

Planning activities

When planning the activities to use in your setting, it is important to be aware of the intended learning. If you know what you hope to achieve with an activity, you can tailor your teaching and assessment processes, collect the necessary resources and consider appropriate language to use. The activities are designed to allow children to draw on personal, first-hand experiences they may have had. For adults who know little about a particular celebration, there are plenty of story and information books suggested in the resources section to refer to.

Planning focused learning

Although all the activities in this book have been tried and tested already, you should always test them yourself before incorporating them into your curriculum. You will then be able to tailor the activities for your particular group of children. If the activity involves only a limited number of children, always make sure that the other children in the setting are occupied and constantly supervised by adults. The following list contains practical suggestions for preparing activities:

• Ensure that the area is both safe and suitable for the purpose. If the activity involves dancing, for example, there must be enough space for children to move freely without bumping into obstacles.

• Look at the activity and decide what resources you will need. Give the children enough materials so that they have a choice of colours, sizes and so on to use.

• You should have somewhere to put all finished products. Lanterns, for example, can be displayed on the window ledge and paintings can be left on a drying rack before they are hung on the wall.

• Check that all implements you plan to use are fit for their intended task. Pencils should be sharpened and paint brushes should be cleaned. If using scissors, make sure they are sharp enough and that, where appropriate, you have some pairs suitable for left-handed children.

• When children are doing messy activities which involve materials such as paint or papier-mâché, make sure they wear messy-play aprons to protect their clothes. You may like to colour code aprons so that, for example, children wear blue for water play, red for painting and so on.

After each activity, encourage children to tidy up. Boxes and shelves for materials should be clearly marked so that children know where items belong. By putting things back in the correct places, children learn the essential mathematical skills of sorting and classifying.

Asking questions

By asking questions and listening carefully to responses, adults can learn much about children's levels of understanding in all areas of development. Adults can ask children two types of question, closed and open. Closed questions tend to require simple, one word answers, such as 'yes' or 'no' and, as such, tell adults little about what the child is thinking. After a while, children may begin to believe that there can be only one correct answer to a question when, in fact, there may be many.

Of much more value to you is the open question. Open questions, such as 'why do you enjoy your birthday?', call on children to think creatively and consider all aspects pertaining to the subject. To reply to an open question, children will need to investigate and review ideas. There can be a whole range of answers to open questions and you can use the responses to learn about children's personal opinions, what they are thinking and how they are feeling. Such questions can also be used to promote self-evaluation, where children are asked to look at their work and, perhaps, comment on ways it could be improved. Open questions also remove the fear of giving a wrong answer and give children the confidence to answer questions in the future. Incorporated in most of the activities in this book are suggested questions that you can ask the children. These are by no means definitive, so take the opportunity to add any others that you see fit.

By listening to and answering the questions posed by adults, children will, naturally, be motivated to take an interest in the world around them, developing a healthy enthusiasm for knowledge. This interest should lead children to develop enquiring minds and to begin asking questions of their own. This, in turn, will lead children to learn to interact, both with other children and with adults. This level of communication will help children to express themselves better, leading them to become more confident and articulate in conversation.

The choice of celebration

Although the celebrations featured in this book are extremely wide-ranging, the list should in no way be seen as definitive. You should use the activities to help plan for all festivals relevant to your setting. Those festivals that appear in this book have been carefully selected so as to represent a broad spectrum of cultures, religions and traditions. This will ensure that the children are exposed to different people and countries from all over the world. The children, it is hoped, will have had a degree of experience in some of the celebrations, thus giving them useful previous knowledge to draw upon and talk about when prompted by adults. It is, therefore, important that you have a good understanding of all of the celebrations yourselves so that you are able to reply with confidence to any question asked. The resources section on page 60 suggests plenty of books that offer background information on all of the celebrations.

It is important that you present the activities to the children in a meaningful context. Where appropriate, you should encourage children to dress up in traditional costume. You should also introduce the celebrations at the time of year that they

traditionally take place. By taking the children to a church during December as part of your Christmas activities, for example, you will be able to show them particular aspects of the celebration, such as the crib, first-hand.

Each of the activities in this book focuses on a particular part of a celebration, such as the theme of weather forecasting for St Swithin's Day. By trying out the activity, children will not only develop particular areas of learning, but they will also be able to use their experiences gained through the activities to recall the celebration. By making a continuous weather chart, for instance, the children will call to mind the legend of St Swithin, as outlined on page 55 in the Cyclopedia of Celebrations. The activities will give them both a better understanding of the wider world and offer them the chance to express themselves through the full range of media.

How to use this book

All About Celebration is divided into six self-contained chapters that develop different aspects of the book's central theme. Each chapter has its own coloured band, to help you identify which chapter you are in, and its own contents list. The contents list gives you a summary of each activity to help you decide which activities to use. The materials needed for each activity are always found at the top left of the activity and the educational aims are underneath.

Educational symbols

Each activity introduces one or more areas of learning. The symbols show you which areas are covered and the accompanying text gives you the specific aims.

 This symbol shows the activity will develop aspects of language and literacy

This symbol shows the activity will develop aspects of creative development

This symbol shows the activity will develop aspects of personal, social and emotional development

 This symbol shows the activity will develop aspects of science and technology

 This symbol shows the activity will develop aspects of mathematics

 This symbol shows the activity will develop aspects of physical development

 This symbol shows the activity will develop aspects of time and place

Each activity is numbered for easy reference.

The triangle and circle show you the suggested adult–child ratio for the activity.

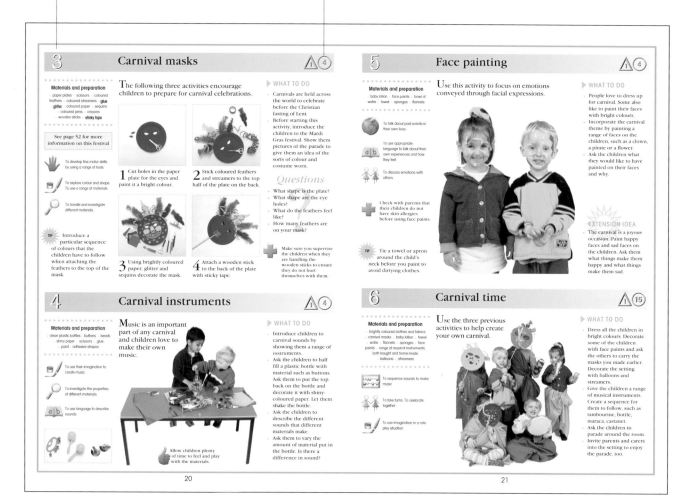

Additional symbols

Many activities have additional hints and tips or safety points. They are identified by the symbols shown below.

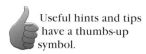 Useful hints and tips have a thumbs-up symbol.

 Safety points have a red cross symbol.

Breaking down the information

Each activity either has step-by-step instructions or bullet-pointed instructions under the heading 'What To Do'. Many activities also have suggested questions and extension ideas, also under the appropriate headings.

 TIP One or more helpful suggestions for increasing an activity's learning value have a star symbol.

Topic web

Each activity in this book is underpinned by one or more areas of learning. This topic web lists all the activities that develop each area of learning under the appropriate heading. Use this web when planning your curriculum to ensure the activities you use develop all areas of learning according to the particular early-years guidelines you are following. This will help you create an educationally exciting and balanced theme that your children will love!

PHYSICAL DEVELOPMENT

PERSONAL, SOCIAL AND EMOTIONAL DEVELOPMENT

SCIENCE AND TECHNOLOGY

CREATIVE DEVELOPMENT

MATHEMATICS

LANGUAGE AND LITERACY

TIME AND PLACE

WHAT IS A CELEBRATION?

This chapter focuses on the role of the early-years professional in preparing activities based around celebration. The importance of dressing up, using meaningful props and giving children first-hand experiences to help them learn are all highlighted. Guidance is given on ways to approach educational visits outside the setting and on the valuable role that can be played by visitors coming into the setting. The activities in this chapter form the basis for all the activities that appear later in the book.

Activities in this chapter

1
Reading stories
Guidance is given on good practice in story reading, such as the kinds of book to read and what language to use

2
Using story props
How to employ props to stimulate interest and aid understanding

3
Dressing up
By dressing up in different costumes from around the world, children can enter into the spirit of celebration

4
Cards and invitations
In this activity, children practise their emergent writing skills and are shown how to work with a range of materials

5
Celebrating birthdays
Children learn that different cultures have different ways of celebrating birthdays

6
Party games
Using games in the setting as an extremely useful way of approaching all areas of learning

7
Visitors to the nursery
Children will learn more about different faiths and celebrations through presentations by relevant visitors

8
Educational visits
Important points to consider before taking children on visits outside the setting are highlighted here

9
Preparing for visits
Be sure to research a venue before taking children, to ensure it is relevant and suitable

10
Celebrating achievements
It is important to display and celebrate children's work to encourage them to take pride in their achievements

1 Reading stories

Materials and preparation

· wide range of appropriate books to support the theme of celebration. Big Books are ideal

 To improve listening and reading skills. To extend experiences through literature and information texts

 To encourage children to take turns

 To extend knowledge of other societies

Use this activity to improve your story reading skills.

👍 Read stories to small groups of children, so they all have a chance to contribute.

▶ WHAT TO DO

· Make sure that you hold the book up so that all the children can see both the words and the pictures.

· Read books with vocabulary that children can understand and that challenges them.

· Ask the children questions about the story you are reading. Use open questions that require more than single word answers.

· If children appear to be distracted or uninterested in the story, look at possible reasons why. Is the language too easy/difficult? Is the book too small for all the children to see? Is there too much text and not enough pictures? Are you encouraging the children to contribute enough?

---

2 Using story props

Materials and preparation

· story props · dressing up clothes range of story books

 To use their imagination in role-play situations

 To develop awareness of how other cultures dress and act

 To sort and classify items according to set criteria

 To recall the events and sequencing of a narrative

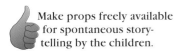 👍 Make props freely available for spontaneous story-telling by the children.

Use props to stimulate interest and help children to understand and retell stories.

▶ WHAT TO DO

· A story prop is a representation of an object that is referred to in a story.

· Read a story to the children and then collect relevant props.

· Re-read the story, giving each child a different prop. When their prop appears in the story ask the children to hold it up in the air.

· Children may like to dress up as the characters in a story and act out the scenes as they appear in the book.

· Make sure you have a range of stories that represent cultures across the world.

Dressing up

Dressing up encourages children to enter into the spirit of celebration.

Materials and preparation

dressing up clothes · masks · face paints · baby lotion · cotton wool

 To learn about other cultures

 To act out real life through role play

 Always get parents' permission before using face paints as some children may have allergies.

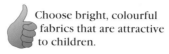 Choose bright, colourful fabrics that are attractive to children.

Using baby lotion before applying face paints makes the paint easier to remove.

Questions

- On what occasions do you wear special clothes?
- What do you wear when you dress up?
- Can you think of any occasions that require other people to dress up?

▶ WHAT TO DO

- Investigate the sorts of clothes that different cultures wear for various celebrations and ask the children to dress up accordingly.
- You can get children to make clothes and masks based around celebrations for role-play activities.
- You may like to re-enact a festival or celebration that involves painting children's faces.

4

Cards and invitations

Making cards and invitations helps develop children's emergent writing skills.

Materials and preparation

coloured paper · scissors · glue paint · paint brushes · crayons pencils · coloured pens · examples of cards and invitations

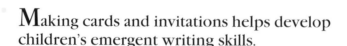 To practise emergent writing for real purposes

 To use scissors appropriately and with increasing control

 To explore and use a range of art materials

Always be aware of each child's first language so that they feel their language is valued and used.

 Always ensure that you have left-handed scissors available for those who need them.

▶ WHAT TO DO

- Provide a wide range of tools for children to write with and varied materials to write on.
- Show children how to make basic cards and invitations. Show them what to write.
- Become role models for the children. If they see an adult writing they will often try to copy.
- It is important that staff praise the children's work as much as possible. They need to feel that their written work is valued and used. Send the cards to families and friends of the setting.

Celebrating birthdays

Materials and preparation

thin card · tissue paper · scissors · glue · streamers · chair

 To talk about past events in own lives

 To take turns. To introduce the idea of giving. To experience the pleasures of celebrating

 To learn to count. To record time passing

TIPS In Germany, children are given a candle marked off with lines and numbers. On each birthday the candle is allowed to burn to the next line. Birthdays in Sweden start with breakfast in bed. Your morning drink is served in a special birthday cup and you are given a piece of cloth with happy birthday written on it.

Make birthday celebrations stand out in your setting by adopting celebrations from different cultures.

 During the year, make sure that everyone has a chance to celebrate their birthday.

If using lighted candles on a birthday cake, keep both the candles and the matches out of reach of children.

WHAT TO DO

- This celebration is based on a traditional Israeli birthday.
- Using a strip of thin card and tissue paper, make a wreath of flowers.
- Decorate a chair with similar tissue paper flowers and coloured streamers.
- Ask the birthday child to sit on the chair whilst the other children sing a birthday song.
- You may like to give the birthday child a present or card.

Questions

- What did you do on your last birthday?
- Can you think of any other celebrations where you give presents?
- Do you know anyone who lives in another country? How do they celebrate their birthdays?

Party games

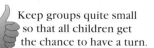

Materials and preparation

chairs · cassette recorder

 To learn to identify items using their names

 To move quickly and with increasing control

 To play with other children

 To remember sequences and counting patterns

 Look in 'This Little Puffin' for further ideas of games to play with the children.

Different party games can help develop different areas of learning.

TIP Expand the 'I Spy' game. For example, 'I spy with my little eye something that rhymes with ...'

WHAT TO DO

- Encourage the children to play a wide range of different games, both inside and outside. Some children will be better at some games than others. It is, therefore, important to vary the activities so that all children can experience success.
- Include games that employ language skills, such as 'I Spy', those that use physical skills, such as 'Musical Chairs' and those that rely on memory and sequences, such as 'The Parson's Cat'.

 Keep groups quite small so that all children get the chance to have a turn.

Visitors to the nursery

To be aware of cultures and beliefs other than their own

To engender a feeling of community

To hear a wide range of stories from many cultures

Try to invite someone in to talk about each event that you plan to celebrate. Parents are often a good source of knowledge.

TIP Ask the visitor to present the subject to small groups of five or six children over the day so that they feel closely involved. This way children can also touch and play with any objects brought in.

Invite visitors into the nursery to talk about aspects of different faiths and cultures.

- The celebrations in this book are drawn from a wide range of faiths and cultures. To help children understand more about each celebration, invite visitors from the relevant communities to come in and talk to the children.
- Let the visitors know what you will be celebrating. Ask them to use simple language when talking to the children and to use visual props as much as possible.
- Prepare the children for the visit in advance. By giving them an introduction to the subject they will find the visit more interesting and, therefore, beneficial.

Educational visits

TIPS Make sure the transport you are taking has enough seatbelts for all the children and adults.
- Ensure that the place you are visiting is suitable for small children.
- First visit yourself and check that there is adequate provision of toilets and washing facilities.
- If you are visiting over the course of a day, you may want to ask parents to prepare lunch for their children.

You must inform parents in writing if you plan to take the children on class outings.

- Before taking children on educational visits outside the setting, write a letter to parents telling them the purpose of the visit and what you hope to achieve. The letter should also say what time you are leaving, how you are getting there, what the children will need to bring and what they need to wear.
- It is essential to have a parental consent form that parents or carers sign before their child is taken off the premises.

Make sure that you have a high adult–child ratio.

Preparing for visits

Materials and preparation

pictures of different places of worship

To show an awareness of different faiths

To recognise real objects from their pictures

Visits play an important role in learning about different faiths.

EXTENSION IDEA

- Take photographs of the visit and ask children to draw pictures of things that remind them of the day out. Stick the photographs and pictures into a home-made class book to record your visit.

▶ WHAT TO DO

- Before taking children on an educational visit, introduce them to the subject by talking to them and showing them pictures of relevant buildings and artefacts. Children will then be able to recognise certain features when on the visit.
- Go on a preliminary visit to check for suitability. If tickets are required for the visit, it may be necessary to book them in advance.
- Make sure parents are fully informed about the visit and have given consent (see Educational Visits (8) page 16).

TIP Try to arrange your visit around the time of the festival or event that you are going to celebrate. The place you are visiting may then be decorated appropriately.

Celebrating achievements

Materials and preparation

piece of work that the child is particularly proud of or enjoys talking about

To promote effective communication.
To raise self-esteem

To promote and extend oral discussion

TIP Always allow children to finish what they are working on, even if it seems to be taking a long time. If this is not possible, carefully clear away the work and put it out again later for the child to finish as soon as possible.

It is important for children to see that their work is valued so that they take pride in their achievements.

▶ WHAT TO DO

- When children finish a piece of work, let them put their name on it and display it on the wall. Displays are excellent ways of keeping parents informed of their children's progress and interests.
- Always praise children's efforts and listen carefully to their views and explanations.
- During quiet times and informal conversations, ask children to complete the sentence 'I'm really good at...' Ask the children to comment on their friends work, too, 'Jamie's really good at ...'

SPRING CELEBRATIONS

This chapter uses festivals and celebrations that fall in Spring as a basis for all the activities. Children are given the opportunity to put together displays in both two and three dimensions, allowing them to develop both their physical and creative skills. All the activities are designed to give children a real feel for the celebrations, many of which are introduced through dressing up and role play. Children learn songs and respond to rhyme through actions. The relevant safety and environmental issues are also highlighted.

Activities in this chapter

1
Japanese doll festival
Children bring dolls into the setting
to form a display

2
Baby clinic
This activity uses a song as a basis to set up a baby clinic.
Children learn the importance of caring for others

3
Carnival masks
A step-by-step activity to making
carnival masks

4
Carnival instruments
Making musical instruments out of old
plastic bottles and different fillings

5
Face painting
Continuing the carnival theme, children have their
faces painted and talk about emotions

6
Carnival time
Children dress up and use masks and face paints from
preceding activities to re-enact a carnival

7
Easter
Sing the hot cross bun song with the children
to help introduce the theme of Easter

8
Easter plants
Looking at spring flowers planted in the setting,
talking to the children about new life

9
Decorating eggs
Children develop their creative skills by making
and decorating papier-mâché eggs

10
Easter egg tree
In this final Easter activity, children hang their eggs
on a branch to create an Easter egg tree

11
Holi
Books and props are used to introduce the
Hindu festival of Holi to the children

12
Splatter hand prints
In this activity children apply paint using
tools other than brushes

13
Eid-ul-Fitr cards
Emergent writing and creative skills are extended
by making traditional greeting cards

14
Celebrations for Eid
Taking Eid as a start, children learn about
the moon and space

Japanese doll festival

Materials and preparation
- selection of dolls preferably from a range of cultures · table

See page 52 for more information on this festival

 To develop fine motor skills by dressing dolls

 To participate in question-and-answer sessions

 To understand that objects can represent real life

 To sort and arrange in order according to set criteria

This activity is based around the Japanese doll festival, Hina Matsuri.

EXTENSION IDEA
- Once you have collected the dolls together, you could ask the children to sort them according to certain criteria, such as the colour of their hair, the colour of their clothes or in order of height.

▶ WHAT TO DO
- Every year, at the Hina Matsuri festival, young girls set up a display of ornamental dolls.
- Try to get dolls from as wide a range of cultures as possible. Form a display with the dolls on top of a table or on a window ledge.
- If possible, find a doll that you can dress and undress. Encourage the children to put clothes on the doll.

TIPS To avoid stereotyping, ensure boys are actively encouraged to participate in this activity.
- Invite fathers to come in with their babies to help demonstrate their roles caring for children.
- Ask children to bring in dolls from home.

---

2 Baby clinic

Materials and preparation
- selection of dolls · moses basket · bandages · scales · leaflets · doctors' and nurses' uniforms

 To listen and respond to rhyme

 To care for others who are sick

 To use imagination to think up actions to accompany a song

The Hina Matsuri dolls were traditionally used to ward off bad luck and illness. Use dolls from the previous activity to set up a baby clinic.

Miss Polly had a dolly

Miss Pol-ly had a dol-ly who was sick, sick, sick so she

called for the doctor to be quick, quick, quick; the

doc-tor came with his bag and his hat, and he

knocked on the door with a rat-a - tat tat

▶ WHAT TO DO
- Sing the song with the children. Ask them to incorporate an action for each line, such as folding their arms and rocking a pretend doll.
- Add another verse: *He looked at the dolly, and he shook his head And he said 'Miss Polly, put her straight to bed.' He wrote on a paper for a pill, pill, pill 'That will make her better, yes it will, will, will!'*
- Invite a health visitor into the setting to talk to the children about what happens in a baby clinic.

3 Carnival masks

Materials and preparation

• paper plates • scissors • coloured feathers • coloured streamers • glue • glitter • coloured paper • sequins • coloured pens • crayons • wooden sticks • sticky tape

See page 52 for more information on this festival

 To develop fine motor skills by using a range of tools

 To explore colour and shape. To use a range of materials

 To handle and investigate different materials

TIP Introduce a particular sequence of colours that the children have to follow when attaching the feathers to the top of the mask.

The following three activities encourage children to prepare for carnival celebrations.

1 Cut holes in the paper plate for the eyes and paint it a bright colour.

2 Stick coloured feathers and streamers to the top half of the plate on the back.

3 Using brightly coloured paper, glitter and sequins decorate the mask.

4 Attach a wooden stick to the back of the plate with sticky tape.

▶ **WHAT TO DO**

• Carnivals are held across the world to celebrate before the Christian fasting of Lent.
• Before starting this activity, introduce the children to the Mardi Gras festival. Show them pictures of the parade to give them an idea of the sorts of colour and costume worn.

Questions

• What shape is the plate?
• What shape are the eye holes?
• What do the feathers feel like?
• How many feathers are on your mask?

Make sure you supervise the children when they are handling the wooden sticks to ensure they do not hurt themselves with them.

4 Carnival instruments

Materials and preparation

• clean plastic bottles • buttons • beads • shiny paper • scissors • glue • paint • adhesive shapes

 To use their imagination to create music

 To investigate the properties of different materials

 To use language to describe sounds

Music is an important part of any carnival and children love to make their own music.

Allow children plenty of time to feel and play with the materials.

▶ **WHAT TO DO**

• Introduce children to carnival sounds by showing them a range of instruments.
• Ask the children to half fill a plastic bottle with material such as buttons. Ask them to put the top back on the bottle and decorate it with shiny-coloured paper. Let them shake the bottle.
• Ask the children to describe the different sounds that different materials make.
• Ask them to vary the amount of material put in the bottle. Is there a difference in sound?

Face painting

Materials and preparation
- baby lotion • face paints • bowl of water • towel • sponges • flannels

To talk about past events in their own lives

To use appropriate language to talk about their own experiences and how they feel

To discuss emotions with others

Check with parents that their children do not have skin allergies before using face paints.

TIP Tie a towel or apron around the child's neck before you paint to avoid dirtying clothes.

Use this activity to focus on emotions conveyed through facial expressions.

▶ **WHAT TO DO**
- People love to dress up for carnival. Some also like to paint their faces with bright colours.
- Incorporate the carnival theme by painting a range of faces on the children, such as a clown, a pirate or a flower.
- Ask the children what they would like to have painted on their faces and why.

EXTENSION IDEA
- The carnival is a joyous occasion. Paint happy faces and sad faces on the children. Ask them what things make them happy and what things make them sad.

6

Carnival time

Materials and preparation
- brightly coloured clothes and fabrics • carnival masks • baby lotion • towel • water • flannels • sponges • face paints • range of musical instruments, both bought and home-made • balloons • streamers

To sequence sounds to make music

To take turns. To celebrate together

To use imagination in a role-play situation

Use the three previous activities to help create your own carnival.

▶ **WHAT TO DO**
- Dress all the children in bright colours. Decorate some of the children with face paints and ask the others to carry the masks you made earlier. Decorate the setting with balloons and streamers.
- Give the children a range of musical instruments. Create a sequence for them to follow, such as tambourine, bottle, maraca, castanet.
- Ask the children to parade around the room.
- Invite parents and carers into the setting to enjoy the parade, too.

7 Easter

Materials and preparation

hot cross buns • oven • reference books on Easter (see resources section)

See page 53 for more information on this festival

 To talk about events in the past

 To understand how materials can change when heated. To express the difference between hot and cold

 To share food as a celebration

EXTENSION IDEA

- Eating hot cross buns is an English custom. Find out how Easter is celebrated elsewhere and introduce these customs to your setting.

Use this poem about hot cross buns to introduce the theme of Easter.

Hot cross buns

Hot cross buns, hot cross buns

One a pen-ny, two a pen-ny, hot cross buns

If you have no daughters, give them to your sons

One a pen-ny, two a pen-ny, hot cross buns

WHAT TO DO

- Show the children the buns and tell them that the cross reminds Christians that Jesus died and came back to life to be with them again.
- Talk to the children about the Easter story. Introduce the idea of helping others.
- Ask the children to feel and smell the buns then put them in the oven to heat. Ask the children to feel and smell the buns again and to talk about any differences they notice. Let them eat the buns. Ask them what they taste like.

Make sure children take care not to burn themselves on the buns. Keep children away from the hot oven. Check for allergies, such as gluten intolerance.

---

8 Easter plants

Materials and preparation

Easter plants • paper • paint • coloured pens • coloured pencils • plenty of tissues

 To respect and develop awareness of nature

 To use comparative language

 To learn about the different parts of a plant

This activity focuses on the theme of new life associated with Easter.

Questions

- Can you think of anything else associated with spring?
- Have you ever seen a newly born animal?

WHAT TO DO

- Find some Easter plants, such as daffodils and crocuses, close to your setting. Look at the plants with the children and name each different part for them, such as the leaves, stamen and petals.
- Encourage the children to feel the smooth petals and the rougher leaves. Ask them to comment on the differences.
- Ask the children to look at the flowers and then draw or paint them.

22

Decorating eggs

Materials and preparation

• strips of old newspaper • water • plain flour • lengths of string • wax crayons • paint • messy-play aprons

To learn that some animals lay eggs

To make objects using a growing range of materials. To talk about colour and texture

EXTENSION IDEA

• Crack one egg open into a bowl. Ask the children to comment on the colour and texture of the egg. Boil one egg, peel it and then show it to the children. Ask them to comment on any changes they notice.

Continue the theme of new life at Easter by making decorative eggs with the children.

Make sure the children do not eat any raw egg.

▶ WHAT TO DO

• You will need to prepare this activity in advance. Mould some egg shapes for the children using papier-mâché. As you stick the paper together, insert a piece of string in the middle leaving a length of about 15 cm hanging out the top.
• Boil some eggs for ten minutes and then leave them to cool.
• Show the children the eggs and encourage them to decorate them.

Questions

• What animals lay eggs?
• Do you know of any animals other than birds that lay eggs? e.g. crocodiles and snakes.
• Are there any other sorts of egg that you would asssociate with Easter?

Easter egg tree

Materials and preparation

• branch • plant pot • stones • soil • home-made decorative eggs

To use language to desribe branches

To develop fine motor skills by delicately hanging the eggs

To respect the environment

Always make sure that children wash their hands after handling dirty branches, stones and soil.

Extend the activity above by hanging brightly decorated eggs from a branch.

Always try to find a fallen branch rather than breaking one off a living tree.

▶ WHAT TO DO

• Find a branch that has fallen from a tree. Make sure it has lots of off-shoots. Fix the branch in a plant pot using stones and soil. Hang the eggs from the branch and display it in a prominent position in the setting.
• You may like to make a selection of these displays using branches from different trees.
• Ask the children to talk about the branches, describing their colour, shape and form. Introduce appropriate language such as bendy, soft, spiky and so on.

Holi

See page 53 for more information on this festival

 To understand that people have different ways of celebrating festivals

 To talk about colour

 To talk about past events in their own lives

EXTENSION IDEA

- When you celebrate Holi, ask the children to come into the setting wearing clothing in colours such as red, green or orange. You can then recreate the colour splashing without having to deal with the mess.

The wheat-harvest festival of Holi in India is sometimes called the Festival of Colour.

TIP Make sure you have books and visual props about the festival for the children to look at and use as reference (see resources section).

▶ WHAT TO DO

- Use this activity to introduce the festival of Holi to the children.
- If there are any Hindu children in your setting, ask them to tell the others what happens in their family during Holi. Do they have a bonfire and do they splatter each other with brightly coloured paint? Ask the children if they can think of any other times in the year that they have bonfires (see Guy Fawke's (9) page 39).
- Invite a visitor into the setting (see Visitors to the nursery (7) page 16) to talk to the children about the festival. Ask the visitor to bring in props where appropriate.

Splatter hand prints

 To use imagination to create patterns

 To handle a ball with control

 To investigate the changes that occur when water is added to powder

This activity can be used to form a Holi display in the setting.

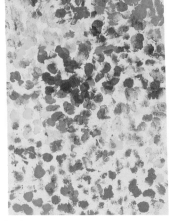

TIP This messy activity is best done outside. Make sure you do it in a large, open space well away from any windows or walls.

▶ WHAT TO DO

- Mix up some yellow, red, orange and green powder paints. Ask the children to dip their hands in the paint and then print them onto paper. Encourage the children to create patterns.
- Using the same colours, dip tennis balls into the paints. Ask the children to drop the balls onto paper from varying heights. Ask them if they notice anything different when the paint splatters.
- Lay the prints flat to dry before putting them up on display.

13   Eid-ul-Fitr cards

Materials and preparation
- coloured card • scissors
- coloured paper • glue • coloured pens and pencils

See page 53 for more information on this festival

 To be aware of other cultures

 To develop emergent writing skills and learn about different writing systems

 To explore and use a wide range of materials

 To look at different shapes and designs

This activity will help to develop children's emergent writing skills.

▶ WHAT TO DO

- The Muslim festival of Eid celebrates the end of the fasting of Ramadan.
- Show the children an example of an Eid greeting card. Now show them an Easter greeting card and ask them to point out any differences.
- Children will see that Eid cards open from left to right. Ask the children to make Eid cards decorated with geometric patterns (Muslims are forbidden from making images of living things).

 See Cards and invitations (4) page 14 for more information.

14   Celebrations for Eid

Materials and preparation
- 2 pieces of wood • strong sticky tape • stiff card • yellow paint • tin foil • play dough • string

 To explore shape in two and three dimensions

 To recognise features of the natural world

Use Eid celebrations to introduce the subject of the moon and space.

See the resources section for reference material on the moon.

Questions
- How do we get to the moon?
- Do you think it takes longer to go to the moon than to go home at the end of the day? How long do you think it takes?
- Do you know any songs or rhymes about the moon?

▶ WHAT TO DO

- Explain that Muslims fast during Ramadan and that the sighting of the new moon signifies the end of fasting and the start of the celebrations for Eid.
- Make a mobile depicting the four phases of the moon. Introduce language such as full moon, crescent moon and so on. You can make the mobile either in two dimensions using card, or in three dimensions using Plasticine or play dough painted yellow or covered with tin foil.
- Explain that the moon looks light because of the sun reflecting off its surface.
- Talk about different aspects of space. Explain that our light comes from the sun.

SUMMER CELEBRATIONS

Festivals and celebrations that fall during Summer form the basis for all the activities in this chapter. Guidance on how to develop all areas of learning is given, from improving physical skills by dancing, to expanding imagination and creativity through role play. Many of the activities require children to work and play alongside others, helping them to understand the importance of co-operation and tolerance. The activities offer plenty of opportunity for learning outdoors, so be sure to seek permission from parents or carers before taking children outside the setting.

Activities in this chapter

1
Çocuk Bayrami
Looking at and choosing appropriate clothes for dressing up

2
Çocuk dance
An extension activity, celebrating the festival by dancing and eating traditional snacks

3
World Environment Day
Through planting seeds, children begin to learn to take a positive interest in the natural environment

4
Story time
Children listen to a story outside that focuses on the importance of trees to the environment

5
Litter hunt
Collecting litter outside shows children the importance of caring for the environment

6
Recycling
Sorting pre-selected materials to show what can and cannot be recycled

7
Midsummer Day
Reading books about witches and fairies may inspire children to try creating their own stories

8
Midsummer dressing up
An imaginative role-play activity where children act out a story

9
Canada Day
Flags are used as a starting point for discussion about colour, shape and design

10
Canadian flag
Making a Canadian flag using leaf-printing techniques

11
Independence Day
A picnic in the setting prompts discussion about food around the world

12
Bell ringing
Learning to follow and create sequences through ringing bells

13
St Swithin's Day
Using a popular legend to introduce the topic of weather

14
Weather forecasting
This activity continues the weather theme by creating a pretend television broadcast

1   Çocuk Bayrami

WHOLE GROUP

Materials and preparation
- reference books (see resources section) · wide selection of appropriate clothes

See page 54 for more information on this festival

To be able to dress with more confidence

To work closely with others. To celebrate the role of children in society

To take part in role play

Let the children dress up to celebrate the Turkish children's festival of Çocuk Bayrami.

TIPS
- See Dressing up (3) page 14 for guidance in this activity.
- Encourage children to help each other to dress up by tying sashes and putting on headgear.

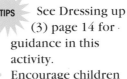

▶ WHAT TO DO
- Ask the children to dress up. Turkish children often wear their national costumes to celebrate this festival. Clothes worn include kaftans, head scarves, waistcoats and baggy trousers.
- Show the children pictures of Turkish clothes from the books listed in the resources section. Ask the children to select appropriate clothes from the dressing-up box.

---

2   Çocuk dance

WHOLE GROUP

Materials and preparation
- dressing-up clothes · Turkish music · cassette recorder · Turkish snacks

To co-operate with others

To move in a sequence and with increasing confidence

To listen to and accurately carry out instructions

Use this activity as an extension to (1) above, and focus on children's physical development.

Check with parents that children have no allergies before giving them any snacks to eat. Burma, for instance, contain nuts.

▶ WHAT TO DO
- Once the children are dressed up, stage a Çocuk Bayrami celebration in the setting. Teach the children a simple dance that involves them following a sequence of movements. Ask them, for example, to hold their arms out and take two steps forward, then one step back, followed by a small jump. If possible, get hold of some Turkish music to play in the background.
- Buy or make traditional Turkish snacks such as simit, burma or kofte for the children to eat.

EXTENSION IDEAS
- Scouts in Turkey plant trees during the festival. Introduce this idea and relate it to World Environment Day (3) page 28.
- Plant some acorns in yoghurt pots and donate the small oaks to a local park.

World Environment Day

Materials and preparation

· plant pots · soil · selection of seeds
· child-sized gardening tools

See page 54 for more
information on this event

 To treat living things with care

 To be able to talk about plant
growth and change

 To handle gardening tools
appropriately

 To keep records and charts
over time

Always make sure that
children wash their
hands after playing
with soil.

Settings without gardens
should supply large tubs
for children to grow
plants in.

Go outside and look at the range of plants. Talk about their importance to the environment.

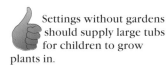

EXTENSION IDEA

· You may like to put together a wall chart that plots the growth and changes in the plants. Use the children's pictures and words describing the growth process and record the days and weeks on the chart.

▶ WHAT TO DO

· World Environment Day happens once a year and is designed to heighten people's respect and care for the environment.
· Plant seeds inside in small pots or outside as appropriate. Involve the children in all aspects of the planting.
· Over the course of the weeks give each child a chance to water the plants and comment on their progress. Here they will be able to use mathematical language to talk about height and learn important new vocabulary related to plants.
· When the plants have grown sufficiently indoors, carefully replant them in the garden or in outside tubs. Continue monitoring them and encourage the children to comment on any changes.

Story time

Materials and preparation

· 'After the Storm' (see resources section)

 To understand the importance of the environment

 To listen and respond to stories. To enjoy pictures and literary language

 To use comparative language and language of size and estimation

Questions

· Which is the tallest tree you can see in the park?
· Can you find any small branches that have been blown down by the wind?

Read 'After the Storm' by Nick Butterworth to continue the theme of World Environment Day.

▶ WHAT TO DO

· Take the children to a local park so that they are outside amongst growing things. Sit down under a tree and read the story to them.
· Talk to them about trees and how important they are for wildlife such as birds, squirrels and butterflies. Talk about natural forces like wind, thunder and lightning.

 Ask a real park keeper to talk to the children about how he cares for the environment. Ask if you can take some branches, dried seed heads and so on back to the setting.

Litter hunt

Materials and preparation

· litter bins · plastic gloves

 To foster a sense of responsibility towards nature

 To sort according to set criteria

To encourage respect for other people

While you are out in the setting's outdoor area, encourage children to pick up safe litter.

▶ WHAT TO DO

· Check that there is no dangerous litter, such as broken glass in your setting.

· Plant some 'safe' litter, such as empty crisp packets and waste paper in your setting. Talk about the importance of keeping your environment clean and highlight the point by asking the children to collect the litter and put it in the litter bins.

Questions

· What do you use bins for?
· What should you do if you see glass on the floor in the park?
· Why should you avoid leaving glass on the floor?

EXTENSION IDEA

· Give the children a selection of recyclable litter. Ask them to sort it by materials, such as paper, plastic and cardboard.

Stress the dangers associated with broken glass, sharp metal and so on. If the children see any, in the local park for instance, tell them not to touch it and ask them to inform an adult.

Recycling

Materials and preparation

· pre-selected litter from the setting

 To sort according to set criteria

 To listen and respond to instructions

 To understand the importance of recycling

Use this activity as an extension to Litter hunt (5) to introduce recycling to the children.

 Take the children to visit a local recycling point.

▶ WHAT TO DO

· Explain to the children that paper is made from wood and that the earth is running out of the trees that the wood comes from. Introduce the idea to the children that paper and other materials can be broken down and used again. This is called recycling.

· Pre-select some safe litter from the setting's inside bin. Explain to the children what sorts of material can be recycled. Tell the children where they can take their litter to be recycled.

Questions

· Do you recycle at home? What do you recycle?
· Where do you take your paper from home to be recycled?

7   Midsummer Day

Materials and preparation

- book from the 'Meg and Mog' series
- selection of relevant books, such as the 'Winnie the Witch' series and 'A Dark, Dark Tale' (see resources section)

> See page 54 for more information on this festival

 To use imagination to create a story

  To listen and respond to stories. To show awareness of how stories are put together

To take turns

Read a 'Meg and Mog' story to introduce the children to witches in a light-hearted way.

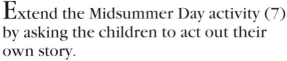 Using a cassette player, record the children's story so they can listen to it later.

▶ WHAT TO DO

- Midsummer Day falls on June 24 and is a time when, according to myth, witches and fairies come out. Inform parents or carers that the topic of witches will be discussed.
- Read a 'Meg and Mog' story to the children. Talk about witches. Underline that fairies and witches are make believe. Continue the theme of witches, fairies and wizards by reading other stories to the children. (see resources section).
- Ask children to make up their own story about witches, fairies and wizards. Ask them to dictate their story to you.

---

8   Midsummer dressing up

Materials and preparation

- home-made story from Midsummer Day (7)
- selection of props such as toy frog, toy spider, witch's clothes, broomstick
- materials to make additional props

 To use their imagination with increasing ability in role play

To be able to work confidently with others

 To respond to actions as directed

Extend the Midsummer Day activity (7) by asking the children to act out their own story.

▶ WHAT TO DO

- Share the story created by the children. Ask the children to suggest items that they would need to act out the story.
- Collect props and appropriate dressing up materials together. Each child could then play a different role in the story.

EXTENSION IDEAS

- Ask the children to make as many of the props as possible, such as a wand, a witch's hat or a pretend broomstick.
- Invite parents and carers in to watch the children act out the story.
- Take photographs of the children acting and use them to illustrate a class book based on the story.

Canada Day

Materials and preparation

- 'Eyewitness – Flag', 'The Usborne Flags Sticker Book' (see resources section)
- paper • paints • coloured pens and pencils

See page 55 for more information on this festival

 To see symbols of other countries

 To be introduced to a range of different shapes

 To use their imagination to design flags of their own

 To use descriptive language of colour and shape

Use a selection of flags to talk to the children about colour, shape and design.

Questions

Introduce appropriate language to describe the shapes in the flag, such as star, stripe, cross and so on.

- Can you spot any colours that appear in more than one flag?
- Have you seen any flags hanging anywhere?
- Where did you see them?

▶ WHAT TO DO

- Canadians display flags every year to mark the founding of their independent nation.
- Show the children a selection of flags from across the world. Ask them if they know what flags are for. Talk about the colours and shapes.
- Ask the children to design flags of their own.

EXTENSION IDEA

- Attach all the made flags to a long piece of string to form a bunting and display it in the setting.

---

10 Canadian flag

Materials and preparation

- maple leaves • white paper
- red paint • paint brushes
- selection of different leaves

 To use different materials for artwork

 To talk about plants

 To talk about and use a range of shapes

Remind the children what the Canadian flag looks like and ask them to print their own.

TIPS Try to find leaves that are still fresh. Dry leaves crumble easily when pressure is applied.
- If you cannot collect leaves, ask the children to use plastic lids, shaped sponges and so on to create imaginary flags.

EXTENSION IDEAS

- Ask children to collect a selection of leaves. Compare the shapes of the different leaves.
- Talk to the children about what tree each leaf has come from.

▶ WHAT TO DO

- Tell children that the shape in the middle of the flag is a maple leaf. If there is a maple tree near the setting, ask children to collect some maple leaves, otherwise collect locally available leaves.
- Ask the children to cover a leaf with red paint and then to print it onto a sheet of white paper. Using the same paint, finish the Canadian flag.

11 Independence Day

Materials and preparation

American food such as pretzels, hot dogs, burgers, popcorn, muffins, waffles and pizza • picnic blanket • paper plates • paper cups • paper napkins • plastic bowls • plastic cutlery

See page 55 for more information on this festival

 To experience other cultures

 To use cutlery with increasing control

 To develop respect for cultural differences

TIPS Ask parents or carers about their family food traditions. Invite them in to prepare dishes for the children to taste.
• Remember to check for allergies before introducing the food.

Introduce Independence Day to the children by having an American-style picnic.

EXTENSION IDEA

• Talk to the children about typical foods from countries around the world such as paella in Spain, sushi in Japan and haggis in Scotland. Use a globe to locate countries around the world.

▶ WHAT TO DO

• On July 4 Americans celebrate gaining their independence from Britain.
• Stage a picnic with popular American food for all the children to enjoy. Talk about the different sorts of food.

12 Bell ringing

Materials and preparation

• selection of different-sized bells

 To respond to instructions

 To understand that different-sized bells make different noises

 To be able to follow a sequence

 To handle an instrument with confidence and increasing control

 Contact your local church or bell ringing society to borrow hand bells.

Liberty Bell was rung to signal the first reading of the Declaration of Independence in 1776.

EXTENSION IDEAS

• Ask older children to repeat the sequence without calling their numbers out. They may even like to create a sequence of their own.
• Arrange a visit to a local church to hear bells rung.

▶ WHAT TO DO

• Make sure you have a selection of hand bells, of differing sizes if possible.
• Give each child a number. Write the numbers on large pieces of card. Create a sequence and ask the children to ring their bell when their number is called out or held up.

St Swithin's Day

Materials and preparation

- large sheet of paper • coloured pens • coloured pencils • coloured card • scissors • thermometer

See page 55 for more information on this festival

 To talk about the weather. To read a thermometer

 To count to 40. To fill in a chart

 To use relevant vocabulary

Questions

- Do you like it when it rains? Why?
- What do you wear when it rains?
- What do you feel like when it is sunny?
- What is your favourite weather?

Celebrating St Swithin's day offers an excellent opportunity to talk about weather.

As weather can change during the day, and because some children only attend for a half-day session, make observations both in the morning and the afternoon.

WHAT TO DO

- According to legend, if it rains on July 15, St Swithin's day, it will rain for the next 40 days.
- Ask the children to help you make a chart for the 40 days following St Swithin's. Each day, take the children outside and ask them to comment on the weather. Fill in all the details on the chart. You may like to make up picture symbols to represent different weather features.
- Show the children how to read a thermometer. Take temperature readings every day and record the readings on the chart. Ask children to tell you, by looking at the chart, how warm it was on a particular day.

Weather forecasting

Materials and preparation

- coloured card • coloured pens • map of Britain • Blu Tac

 To use imagination through role play

 To convey information through language

 To begin to develop an understanding of maps

Extend the St Swithin's Day activity (13) by introducing the children to weather forecasting.

EXTENSION IDEA

- Ask children why they think they need weather forecasts. Discuss how the weather effects what you decide to wear and what activities you are able to do outside.

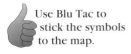 Use Blu Tac to stick the symbols to the map.

WHAT TO DO

- Show the children a televised weather forecast to give them an idea of what happens.
- If you have used pictorial symbols to represent the weather in the chart for the activity above, use the same symbols here, making cut-outs from card.
- Cut out a large picture of Great Britain and stick it on the wall. Ask one child to perform a weather forecast, sticking the symbols to the map as done on television. Ask the child to tell the other children what each symbol means as he is sticking it on.

AUTUMN CELEBRATIONS

Autumn celebrations form the basis for the activities in this chapter. There are plenty of opportunities for children to enrich their language and literacy skills by listening to and looking at stories, songs and poems; suggestions are also given on how to extend activities through role play. Children are helped to follow step-by-step instructions, making both kites and Diwali lamps, so as to support physical, imaginative and creative development. This chapter deals with festivals and celebrations that find their origin in the distant past, thus helping to give children a sense of time and history.

Activities in this chapter

1
Chinese kite poem
Reading a poem to introduce a festival
and to talk about rhyme

2
Making kites
A follow-up step-by-step activity to make kites
using paper bags and string

3
Harvest Festival
Children look at, feel and taste different sorts of
bread as they learn about the harvest

4
Little Red Hen
Using story-prop figures on a felt background,
children retell a well-known story

5
Harvest picnic
Holding a picnic helps children to learn about different sorts of
food and the importance of sharing in an enjoyable way

6
Harvest interest table
Exploring different properties of food, such as
colour, texture and taste

7
Halloween story telling
After hearing a traditional tale, children
talk about Halloween and ghosts

8
Spooky book
Children hear a scary story and are free to
discuss their own emotions of fear

9
Guy Fawkes
Learning about bonfires, children dress up
and pretend to be flames

10
Firework display
In this activity, children listen to a firework poem and
then create their own bonfire collage for display

11
Diwali
By listening to a story, children learn
about the Hindu festival of Diwali

12
Diwali lights
Once they have done this activity, children will
understand one of the main traditions of Diwali

13
Rangoli designs
This creative activity can be done
either inside or outside

14
Diwali cards
Using a range of tools, children develop both their physical
and their emergent writing skills as they
communicate Diwali greetings

1 Chinese kite poem

See page 56 for more information on this festival

Materials and preparation
- kite • 'Follow Jo's Kite', 'Up and Up' storybooks (see resources section)

To learn something about the wind

To listen and respond to a poem. To understand and enjoy rhyme

Read this poem to the children and talk to them about the Chinese Kite Festival.

A kite on the ground
is just paper and string
but up in the air
it will dance and sing.

A kite in the air
will dance and will caper
but back on the ground
is just string and paper.

Anon

▶ WHAT TO DO
- Read the poem to the children. Point out the rhyme on alternate lines
- Ask the children if they have ever seen a kite or if they have one at home. Bring one in for the children to look at.
- Introduce the idea that sometimes small bells are attached to the kites to 'make them sing'.
- Ask the children if they know what makes the kite 'dance'. Talk to them about the wind.

2 Making kites

Materials and preparation
- large paper bags • coloured paint
- ring re-inforcers • string • scissors
- coloured streamers

To handle tools appropriately and with increasing control

To listen to and follow instructions

To create an object using a range of materials

To use a range of mathematical language

Questions
- How many kites can you see?
- Which kite do you like best? Why?
- How many streamers are there on each kite?

This is a good follow-up activity to the Chinese Kite poem above.

1 Paint brightly coloured patterns onto a large paper bag. Leave the bag to dry out.

2 Punch holes in the four corners. Tie one loop on each side by feeding string through the holes.

3 Attach one long piece of string to the two loops at the back of the bag to form a long handle.

4 Stick long lengths of coloured streamers to the bottom of the kite for decoration.

▶ WHAT TO DO
- Once the children have made the kites, take them to a park and let the children try to fly them.

☀ EXTENSION IDEA
- Display all the kites in the setting so they are easy to see and take down for flying outside. Ask the children to look at the kites and to tell you how many different shapes they can see on the designs.

👍 Strengthen the holes on the bag with ring re-inforcers.

Materials and preparation

- selection of breads, such as pitta, ciabatta, focaccia, rye bread, split tin
- grains of wheat • yeast

See page 56 for more information on this festival

 To go shopping and encounter different breads

 To learn that wheat can be turned into bread. To observe the process of yeast rising and baking

 To use comparative language and discuss everyday experiences

 To shop and use money

A pproach the theme of Harvest Festival by bringing different breads into the nursery.

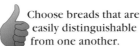 Choose breads that are easily distinguishable from one another.

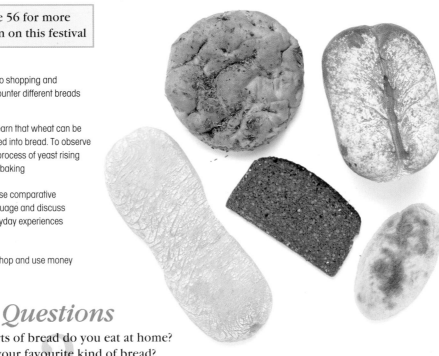

Questions

- What sorts of bread do you eat at home?
- What is your favourite kind of bread?
- Do you make bread at home? Do you notice any differences to the bread you buy in the shop?

Check with parents or carers that their children have no gluten allergies or religious beliefs that prevent them from eating bread.

WHAT TO DO

- Take the children to buy a selection of breads from the bakery. Display the breads and ask the children to comment on any differences they notice between the breads. Invite the children to feel and taste them. What differences do they notice?
- Introduce comparative language such as paler/darker, softer/harder, lighter/heavier.

EXTENSION IDEAS

- Explain that bread is made from wheat and that wheat is harvested from the fields when it is ripe. Show the children some grains of wheat and how it is crushed to make flour. Make bread together.
- Arrange a tour around your local bakers

---

4 Little Red Hen

Materials and preparation

- range of different coloured felt
- scissors • Velcro • 'The Little Red Hen' storybook (see resources section)

 To listen and respond to a story. To re-create a narrative

 To join in group activities led by an adult. To encounter a moral theme in a traditional folk tale

TIP Focus on the harvest theme in the story. Draw the children's attention to the change from seed to wheat, from wheat to flour and from flour to bread.

C reate a storyboard of 'The Little Red Hen' to continue the theme of making bread during harvest.

WHAT TO DO

- Make a storyboard to help tell the story. Cut out pieces of felt to represent elements from the story, such as the hen, or the windmill. Attach Velcro to the back of each piece. Stick felt onto a wooden board to create a background.
- Read the story to the children. Now re-read it and, taking turns, ask the children to stick the pieces of felt onto the storyboard as each element is mentioned in the story. Leave the props available for free play.

Materials and preparation

* range of harvest food such as apples, pears, blackberries, bread, corn-on-the-cob and so on • plastic bowls and plates • picnic blanket

 To discuss the role played by the weather in growing plants

 To encourage sharing and the enjoyment of eating together

TIP Extend children's knowledge by explaining the importance of the weather to the harvest. Explain that crops must have both sun and rain to grow properly.

* Explain that people celebrated the harvest because it meant that they would have food for the coming year.

Harvest festivals often centre around celebratory meals or picnics.

Questions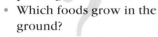

* Which foods at the picnic grow on trees?
* Which foods grow in the ground?
* Which is your favourite food?

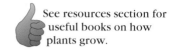 See resources section for useful books on how plants grow.

▶ WHAT TO DO

* Hold a nursery picnic, inside or outside. Include as many harvest foods as possible such as apples, bread, corn-on-the-cob and so on.
* Talk to the children about the importance of giving and sharing.

6   Harvest interest table

Materials and preparation

* table • selection of harvest produce such as apples, plums, parsnips, potatoes, cauliflower and so on

 To talk about a range of natural produce – its colour, taste, texture and origin

 To talk about shape

EXTENSION IDEA

* Invite a keen gardener, farmer or small-holder into the setting to discuss the joys and problems of growing vegetables and fruit.

Using the same sorts of produce as for Harvest picnic (5), set up an interest table.

▶ WHAT TO DO

* Ask the children to bring in foods from home. Stick labels to all the items so that children can identify them by name.

7 Halloween story telling

Materials and preparation

- 'A Dark, Dark Tale' storybook (see resources section)

See page 56 for more information on this festival

 To listen and respond to a traditional tale

 To talk about their emotions – if they wish to do so

 To talk about events in own lives

Questions

- Do you do special things for Halloween?
- Have you ever been 'trick or treating'? What was the best treat you got?
- Can you think of any other stories about ghosts?

Read the traditional tale below to the children to introduce the theme of Halloween.

In a dark, dark wood,
there was a dark, dark house

And in that dark, dark house,
there was a dark, dark room

And in that dark, dark room
there was a dark, dark cupboard

And in that dark, dark cupboard,
there was a dark, dark shelf

And on that dark, dark shelf,
there was a dark, dark box

And in that dark, dark box, there was a **GHOST**

Traditional

▶ WHAT TO DO

- Read this tale to the children. Ask them if they are ever frightened. Let them talk about what frightens them.
- Ask the children if they have ever dressed up as a ghost for Halloween. Ask them what they would dress up as if they had a choice. Ask them why.

---

8 Spooky book

Materials and preparation

- 'The Berenstain Bears and The Spooky Old Tree' storybook (see resources section)

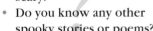 To respond appropriately to questions. To enjoy a story book

 To talk about own experiences. To talk about emotions

EXTENSION IDEA

- Talk about children's own personal experiences of being frightened. Ask the children to suggest things that frighten them.

Extend opportunities to talk about emotions by reading spooky stories.

Questions

- What places do you find scary?
- Do you know any other spooky stories or poems?

▶ WHAT TO DO

- Show the children the cover of the book 'The Berenstain Bears and The Spooky Old Tree'. Ask the children to tell you what they think the story will be about.
- When reading the story, ask the children to respond to the repeated question 'Do they dare?'
- Explain to the children that the bears shiver because they are scared.

Guy Fawkes

Materials and preparation

• lengths of red, orange and yellow material • smoke-coloured streamers

See page 57 for more information on this festival

To move and dance with confidence and increasing control

To use appropriate, descriptive language

To represent an object through action

To learn about danger and the risks of fire

Children dress up and play at being flames to celebrate Guy Fawkes night.

☀ EXTENSION IDEA

• Children may like to use instruments to make sound effects, such as maracas to simulate the twigs crackling.

Be sure to highlight the dangers associated with fire and fireworks.

👍 Ask the children to simulate smoke by waving around appropriately coloured streamers.

▶ WHAT TO DO

• Explain to the children that some people in Britain have bonfires every year on November 5 to commemorate Guy Fawkes night.

• Ask the children what a bonfire looks like. Talk about colours, sounds, sights and smells associated with bonfires.

• Introduce language, such as crackling, hissing, swirling, darting and leaping to describe the different aspects of the burning fire.

• Using lengths of red, orange and yellow material, ask the children to dress up and dance around, simulating the darting and leaping movements of flames. They may like to include relevant sound effects at the same time.

---

10 Firework display

Materials and preparation

• dark blue, brown, red, orange and yellow paper • scissors • coloured felt tipped pens • glue • glitter

To talk about their own experiences

To create a display using a range of materials

To learn about personal safety

TIP Use this activity as an opportunity to teach the children about firework safety. Ask parents or carers to back up such teaching.

Guy Fawkes night is traditionally celebrated with firework displays all over Britain.

Zooming, whirring, whizzing round,

Fireworks raining on the ground.

Golden fountains, Silver Rain

Spurting high – then down again.

Gold and silver in the air;

Don't stand too close and do take care.

Tomato soup and chestnut brown,

Bangers jumping up and down.

Elizabeth Clare

▶ WHAT TO DO

• Explain to the children that many people set off fireworks to remember that Guy Fawkes planned to blow up King James 1 and the Parliament with gunpowder.

• Share the poem and ask the children about their experiences of fireworks.

• Ask the children to help create an indoor firework display on the wall. Make a bonfire using brown paper for logs. Flames can be made out of red, orange and yellow paper. Children can draw fireworks to stick onto the display. They may like to use multi-coloured glitter to represent the fireworks exploding.

Diwali

See page 57 for more information on this festival

 To show an increasing ability to use their imagination

 To listen and respond to stories. To appreciate the stories of other cultures

 To join in group activities led by an adult. To co-operate in role play with each other

Questions

• Do you know anyone who has gone away for a long time and then come back home?
• How do you feel when someone comes home?
• What do you do to celebrate?

Use the story of 'Rama and the Demon King' to introduce the Hindu festival of Diwali and to initiate role-play activities.

▶ **WHAT TO DO**

• Read the story to the children. Talk about the theme of homecoming.
• Ask the children to choose which characters they would like to play such as Rama, Sita or Ravana.
• Ask the children why they want to play a particular character. Ask the children to act out the story as you read it.

EXTENSION IDEA

• Ask children to look at the pictures in the book and then help them to make props and choose costumes from the dressing-up box.

12

Diwali lights

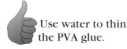

 To use descriptive and comparative language

To understand the properties of different materials

 To use hands to mould clay. To use tools with confidence and increasing control

 Warn the children of the dangers of naked flames. When lit, make sure the lamps are out of the reach of children. Do not allow children to handle matches.

Celebrate Diwali by making your own diva lamps to display on the window ledge.

1 Roll an 8-cm cube of clay into a ball and, with your thumbs, make a small pot with a lip on one side.

2 Using a pencil, score patterns around the pot and glaze it with brightly coloured PVA glue.

▶ **WHAT TO DO**

• Encourage the children to squeeze the clay. Ask them what happens to it.
• Ask the children to describe what the clay feels like. Introduce language such as soft, hard, squidgy, stiff, smooth and so on. Follow steps one and two to make the pots and put tea lights inside them.
• Ask the children to describe any differences they notice after the pots have been glazed.
• Display the finished pots on the window ledge.

Use water to thin the PVA glue.

Rangoli designs

- coloured beads, pebbles and Unifix cubes • powder paint • coloured pens and pencils • paper

 To identify a range of shapes

 To use imagination to create a range of designs

 To work effectively as part of a group

TIPS Try to create the design in a quiet corner so that children do not disturb it when moving round the setting.
- Create one large pattern where a group of children all work together. This will help children to cooperate with others.

Hindus, during Diwali, decorate their floors with brightly coloured patterns, called rangoli.

EXTENSION IDEA

- As it will be difficult to display designs on the floor, ask the children to draw or paint some patterns on paper and stick them up on the wall.

▶ WHAT TO DO

- Ask the children to look at the picture of the rangoli pattern on this page and to identify and name as many different shapes in the pattern as they can.
- Using coloured beads, pebbles and Unifix cubes, ask the children to make their own rangoli design on the nursery floor. Rangoli designs are usually based on flower or leaf shapes.
- If the weather is nice, take the children into the outside play area and ask them to make a similar pattern using coloured powder paints.

 Supervise children using small materials to ensure they do not swallow them.

Diwali cards

- pencil • scissors • glue • coloured card • coloured pens and pencils

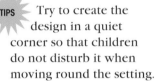 To develop communication and emergent writing

 To use scissors appropriately and with increasing control

 To explore imaginative pattern-making

 See Cards and invitations (4) page 14 for more guidance on this activity

Complete your Diwali celebrations by helping the children make Diwali cards.

EXTENSION IDEAS

- Add suitable greetings to the front of the card, such as 'Subh Diwali' meaning 'Happy Diwali'.
- Invite the children to 'write' their own message inside.

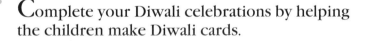

▶ WHAT TO DO

- Help the children draw round and cut out the shape of their hands. Ask the children to stick the shapes to a folded piece of card and decorate them with geometric patterns or flower designs.

WINTER CELEBRATIONS

Chapter five focuses on festivals and celebrations that fall during the winter months. There are activities based on celebrations that children are likely to be familiar with, such as Christmas, and others that draw their inspiration from less well-known festivals, such as Kwanzaa. Certain activities also encourage children to learn about, discuss and show consideration for different animals that they may encounter. There are further opportunities for children to extend their social, physical and mathematical skills by cooking festival foods. You should pay close attention to all the safety tips in order to avoid any accidents in the setting.

Activities in this chapter

1
St Lucia Day
Children dress up in Lucia Day costumes

2
Lucia biscuits
A step-by-step activity to make traditional Lucia biscuits

3
Hannukah
Jewish artefacts and books help children learn about Hannukah

4
Potato latkes
By cooking Jewish snacks, children learn about colour and texture

5
Dreidel game
In this activity, children make and play a Hannukah game

6
Candle song
This song introduces rhyme and teaches sequencing

7
Christmas story
The Christmas story leads children to talk about their families

8
Letter writing
Children use mark-making skills to write letters to Father Christmas

9
Tree decorations
In this activity, children make decorations out of salt dough and talk about their experiences of Christmas

10
Bird feeders
Making bird feeders encourages care and respect for animals

11
Kwanzaa
Children read a Kwanzaa story and share personal memories

12
Big Book
Children make a group book charting recent activities in the setting

13
New Year celebrations
By acting out the story of 'Cinderella' children are helped to extend their imaginative insights into traditional stories

14
Chinese New Year lantern
This activity encourages children to use a range of materials

15
The year of the ...
Using templates, children identify the animals of the Chinese year and make masks for play activities

16
Chinese dragon
In this activity, children make a Chinese dragon and use it to process around the setting

17
Catching the dragon's tail
This game encourages children to follow instructions, have fun and be aware of the space around them

St Lucia Day

See page 58 for more information on this festival

Materials and preparation

· stiff card · evergreen leaves · glue · candles · sticky star shapes · white sheets · red ribbon for sashes

To explore and use a range of materials

To experience other cultures

Use battery-powered candles rather than real ones when making the crown to avoid any potential fire risk.

Celebrate the Swedish festival of Santa Lucia by dressing up in traditional costumes.

▶ WHAT TO DO

· Using card, ask the children to help you make a crown. Attach evergreen leaves to the outside. Stick seven candles around the outside of the crown. Ask the children to make a selection of conical hats out of card and to decorate them with stars.

· Help the children to dress in white robes. Use adult-sized shirts or old sheets. Tie red ribbon sashes around their waists. Ask one girl to wear the crown and the other children to wear the conical hats.

---

2 Lucia biscuits

Materials and preparation

· 100g margarine · 250ml milk · 1g saffron · 1tsp sugar · 25g yeast · pinch of salt · 60–70g caster sugar · 1½ tbsp warm water · 2 eggs · 550-600g plain flour · 60g raisins · pan · wooden spoon · mortar · mixing bowl · baking tray · pastry brush · cooling tray · tea towel

To explore materials and equipment

To use a range of tools appropriately and with increasing control

To use appropriate mathematical language to talk about quantity

To talk about change

Inform parents or carers of the ingredients of the biscuits in case of any allergies.

Do not allow children near the hot oven.

Use this cooking activity to complete your Lucia Day celebrations.

1 Melt the margarine in a pan. Add milk and gently warm. Crush the saffron and sugar and add to the pan.

2 Crumble the yeast in a bowl and add the salt, caster sugar and water. Pour in the saffron milk, add the eggs and mix.

3 Mix the flour and the raisins with the liquid to make dough. Knead it until pliable. Cover the dough.

4 Leave to rise for 1hr 30 mins, then Make small 'S' shapes with the dough. Decorate with raisins. Leave to rise for a further 15 mins.

▶ WHAT TO DO

· Follow steps one to four below. Brush the biscuits with lightly whipped egg and bake at 240ºC (510ºF, Gas mark 9) for 10 mins or until brown. Cover the biscuits with a tea towel and leave to cool on a wire rack.

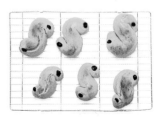

Questions

· What colour is the saffron milk? Can you think of anything else the same colour?

· What does the dough feel like?

· How can we find out how many biscuits we need?

3 Hannukah

Materials and preparation

'Judaism' information book (see resources section) · selection of Jewish artefacts

See page 58 for more information on this festival

 To listen and respond to a story

 To be aware of different beliefs

 See Educational visits (8) page 16 and Preparing for visits (9) page 17 for further guidance.

Hannukah starts on the 25th day of the Jewish month of Kislev.

TIP Invite a member of the local Jewish community to come in to talk to the children about Hannukah and Judaism.

WHAT TO DO

- Tell the children the story of how Hannukah came to be. Show them the book on Judaism.
- If there are any Jewish children in the setting, ask them how they celebrate Hannukah. Try to bring in some Jewish artefacts such as the hannukiya, the candle holder, for children to look at.
- Organise a trip to a local synagogue around the time of Hannukah to give the children a real feel for the festival.

4 Potato latkes

Materials and preparation

4 potatoes · 1 onion · potato peeler · grater · mixing bowl · 1 tbsp flour · 1/2 tbsp baking powder · wooden spoon · 2 eggs · fork to beat eggs · salt and pepper · oil for frying · frying pan · fish slice

 To use meaningful language in context

 To use a range of materials with confidence and increasing control

 To listen, observe and follow instructions

 Do the frying yourself so children do not burn themselves with the hot oil and keep children away from the oven and any hot cooking implements.

 Inform parents or carers of the ingredients in the recipe in case of any allergies.

Make this Hannukah snack of latkes and talk about colour, texture and taste.

1 Peel and wash 4 potatoes and 1 onion. Grate them all and drain off any excess liquid.

2 Mix 1 tbsp of flour with 1/2 tbsp of baking powder. Beat 2 eggs and add to the mixture.

3 Add the onions to the potatoes and season. Mix all the ingredients together.

4 Heat some oil in a frying pan and spoon the mixture on. Cook both sides until brown.

WHAT TO DO

- Ask the children to work together to make potato latkes. Make each child responsible for a different part of the recipe. Demonstrate how to use particular tools first. Closely supervise use of the grater – you may prefer to use a food processor.
- As the children are preparing the recipe, ask them to comment on what they are doing. Introduce meaningful language, such as grating, whisking and frying.

Dreidel game

Materials and preparation

· stiff card · coloured pens · glitter
· glue · cocktail sticks · buttons

 To relate symbols to numbers

 To listen to and follow instructions

 To explore colour and shape

Always supervise children when they are playing with cocktail sticks.

Continue the theme of Hannukah by making a dreidel with the children.

EXTENSION IDEAS

• Play the dreidel game with the children. Use old buttons as tokens. Spin the dreidel and see what symbol it lands on. If it lands on 'put in', the children must put half their tokens in the middle. If it lands on 'win all', the child takes all the tokens in the middle and so on.

▶ WHAT TO DO

· Cut out 10cm x 10cm squares of stiff card for the children. Ask them to copy the four Hebrew symbols drawn on the dreidels shown on this page. Decorate the card with glitter and brightly coloured pens. Ask the children to push a cocktail stick through the centre of the card so that half the stick protrudes from the bottom of the dreidel.

· For the dreidel game, one symbol stands for 'win all', another, 'win half', the next, 'win nothing' and the last 'put in'. Let the children decide which symbol represents which prize and note down their choices.

 Play with small numbers of buttons to make counting easier for all children.

Candle song

Materials and preparation

· 9 candles · hannukiya (Jewish candlestick)

 To listen to and respond to rhyme

 To recognise and continue a sequence

TIPS Consult the section on Hannukah on page 58. Explain to the children why Jews light eight candles during Hannukah. Explain that the ninth candle is for lighting the others.

· Find a hannukiya and light the candles as the children sing the song. Keep candles and flames out of children's reach.

Complete your Hannukah celebrations by asking children to recite the song below.

One little candle burn, burn, burn,
Hannukah is here,

One little candle bright and clear
Hannukah is here.

Two little candles burn, burn, burn
Hannukah is here,

Two little candles bright and clear,
Hannukah is here.

▶ WHAT TO DO

· Read the first two verses of the song to the children. Ask them if they can predict what the next verse will be.

· Ask the children to recite one verse each up to 'Eight little candles'.

7   Christmas story

Materials and preparation
- 'Jesus' Christmas Party' storybook (see resources section) • baby doll • Moses basket

See page 58 for more information on this festival

 To listen and respond to a story. To participate in question and answer sessions

 To talk about their own lives

Use this activity to introduce the Christian story of Christmas to the children.

EXTENSION IDEA
- Explain to the children that, just as they receive presents on their birthday, so we give and receive presents to celebrate Jesus' birthday.

► WHAT TO DO
- Tell the children that Jesus is the son of the Christian God and that the feast of Christmas marks his birthday.
- Tell the Christmas story and explain that Jesus was born in a manger. Ask the children if they know where they were born. Ask if they were born at home, in a hospital and so on. If they have any younger brothers or sisters, ask the children if they can remember when and where they were born.
- Bring in a baby doll for the children to play with. Encourage both boys and girls to play with the doll.

---

8   Letter writing

Materials and preparation
- coloured paper • pens • envelopes • red card • glue • sticky tape

 To encourage emergent writing skills and communication

 To sort and classify according to set criteria

 To understand the importance of giving as well as receiving

By writing a Christmas letter, children will develop their emergent writing skills.

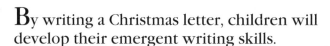

► WHAT TO DO
- Bring in some letters and envelopes. Talk about letter writing. Ask the children what they would like for Christmas and then help them to write their own letters. Scribe for reluctant writers and encourage pictures and pretend writing.

EXTENSION IDEAS
- Help the children to make a post box by using a large cylinder of red card with a slot cut out for posting the letters. Add a cone-shaped lid.
- Set up a sorting office, where children can sort post according to size and colour.
- Talk about the importance of giving as well as receiving presents.
- Using open boxes, set up a pigeon hole system so children can send and receive internal mail.

Tree decorations

Materials and preparation

· mixing bowl · 4 cups of flour · 1 cup of salt · 1½ cups of water · shaped pastry cutters · coloured paint · glitter · ribbon

 To explore and use a range of materials

 To be able to thread ribbon

 To see how materials change when cooked

 To use salt dough to make a range of shapes

This activity shows children how to make Christmas tree decorations using salt dough.

▶ WHAT TO DO

· Ask the children to mix the flour, water and salt together in the mixing bowl using either their hands or spoons.
· Let them sprinkle flour over a chopping board, knead the dough on the board until smooth and cut Christmas shapes out of the salt dough using the shaped pastry cutters. Then follow steps one to three below. If you cannot find suitable-cutters, make card templates to cut around.

1 Make holes in the top of the Christmas shapes. Bake at 170°C (360°F, Gas mark 4), for one hour.

2 Leave the shapes to cool and then decorate with brightly coloured paint.

3 Tie some ribbon through the hole at the top. Add any extra decoration such as glitter.

Materials and preparation

· Christmas tree · material to decorate the base · Christmas lights · home-made Christmas decorations

 To talk about past events in their own lives

 To participate in question and answer sessions

Ask the children to hang the decorations on a Christmas tree.

Questions

· Where have you seen Christmas trees before?
· What do you hang on the tree at home?
· What else do you do at Christmas time that is special?

EXTENSION IDEA

· Read 'Santa's Sackful of Best Christmas Ideas' and 'Festivals' (see resources section) for information on Christmas traditions around the world.

👍 Make sure that the tree is small enough so that all children can reach to hang decorations.

Bird feeders

Materials and preparation

· plastic beaker · square of fine garden netting · unsalted peanuts · string

To observe living things. To talk about observations

To learn how to construct something useful

To learn to treat living things with care and concern

Have some bird reference books so that children can try to match the species that use the feeder to their picture in the book.

Supervise the children during this activity to make sure they do not eat the peanuts.

Some children may have allergies. Do not let children who you know to have allergies near this activity.

In Finland, at Christmas time, people make feeders for birds that have not migrated.

1 Push a square of fine garden netting into a beaker, holding the excess down over the sides.

2 Still holding the netting over the sides, fill the beaker with unsalted peanuts.

 Make sure you use unsalted peanuts. Salted peanuts could kill the birds.

3 Let go of the netting and tie it together with a piece of string. Hang outside near a window.

▶ WHAT TO DO

· Keep a chart of what and how many birds visit the feeder. Ask the children to draw or paint pictures of the different species of bird that visit the feeder. Make a class book.

· Talk to the children about migration. Explain that some birds, during the winter, fly to warmer countries to find food, while many, familiar birds stay here.

11

Kwanzaa

Materials and preparation

· 'The Patchwork Quilt' storybook (see resources section) · patchwork quilt

See page 59 for more information on this festival

To talk about past events

To express own feelings and foster self-esteem

Use the Afro-American festival of Kwanzaa to encourage children to talk about their lives.

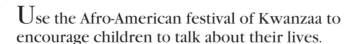

▶ WHAT TO DO

· Read 'The Patchwork Quilt' to the children. The story is about a quilt made by a grandmother and the different memories it holds. Try to get hold of a patchwork quilt for the children to look at. Your local neddlecraft shop may lend you one.

· After listening to the story, ask the children to share their memories of things they have enjoyed doing with their families.

· Ask the children if they can remember things that they did not enjoy doing. Ask them why.

EXTENSION IDEAS

· Ask the children if they have any siblings and to describe them.
· Invite older relatives in to share memories with the children.

12 Big Book

Materials and preparation

- coloured paper and string to make Big Book • examples of children's work

 To cooperate with others

 To sequence events chronologically

 To make a Big Book to promote shared writing and reading

👍 Encourage children to talk about events and activities they have done before you start on the book.

Help the children to compile a Big Book for Kwanzaa, recording recent activities in the setting.

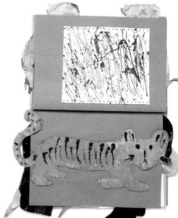

TIP On each page of the book, briefly describe what learning you were trying to achieve with each activity. Parents or carers can then look at the book to gain a better understanding of what their children are doing.

▶ WHAT TO DO

- Make a class Big Book with the children. Stick pictures, photographs and examples of emergent writing into the book. Arrange them in order of when they were done. Write a description next to each activity.
- As the children work on the book, remind them of all the good things they have enjoyed doing together in the setting.
- Give all the children a chance to contribute.

13 New Year celebrations

Materials and preparation

- 'Cinderella' storybook (see resources section) • dressing-up clothes • home-made wand • paper, coloured pens and paint to make a wall display

See page 59 for more information on this festival

 To listen and respond to a traditional story

🎨 To extend imaginative role-play situations

To take turns

Celebrate the New Year by reading about and performing a pantomime.

👍 Invite parents and carers in to watch the pantomime.

"What lovely slippers!" said Cinderella. "Thank you." Then she frowned. "But how am I going to get to the palace?"

The fairy godmother smiled, then pointed her wand at a pumpkin. It changed into a magnificent coach.

▶ WHAT TO DO

- Talk to the children about pantomimes and suggest staging one.
- Share 'Cinderella' with the children and assign them roles to act out the story.
- Leave the book available for the children to read and re-tell.

TIPS Some of the girls in your setting may have ballet or fancy-dress costumes they can bring in. You could use clothes from your dressing-up box or make costumes out of crêpe paper.
- Make a wall display of all the elements of the story, such as the palace, the coach and the pumpkin.

49

14 Chinese New Year lantern

Materials and preparation

- sheet of red paper • paint • wax crayons • glitter • pencil • scissors • glue • thin strip of paper

See page 59 for more information on this festival

 To handle scissors with confidence and increasing control

 To make a display

Questions

- Can you think of any other celebrations that use candles, lamps or lights?
- Have you ever seen a Chinese lantern?
- Where did you see it?
- What are the slits in the lantern for?

The lantern festival traditionally falls on the 13th night of Chinese New Year celebrations.

1 Decorate a sheet of red paper with varied pattern work. Fold the paper in half lengthways.

2 Draw a line about 2 cm from the open edge. Cut slits along the folded edge up to the line.

3 Unfold the paper and roll it around until the short ends meet. Stick the ends to form a cylinder.

4 Cut a thin strip of paper and glue it to the inside of the lamp to make a handle. Leave to dry.

EXTENSION IDEAS

- Either make a display with the lanterns on the window ledge or attach a long piece of string from one side of the setting to the other and hang the lanterns from it.
- Form a procession with the children carrying the lanterns attached to long, wooden poles.

Invite a Chinese member of the community into the setting to draw some characters for the children to copy.

---

15 The year of the ...

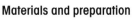

Materials and preparation

- mask templates on pages 62-63
- 30-cm dowelling rods (1 for each mask) • sticky tape

 To talk about themselves

 To use scissors with increasing control

 To identify animals

Follow the activity above by making animal masks to help celebrate Chinese New Year.

▶ WHAT TO DO

- Explain that the Chinese calendar is made up of a 12-yearly cycle and that each year is represented by an animal. Explain that each child's year of birth will be represented by one of these animals. Photocopy, enlarge and cut out the animal mask templates on pages 62-63. Let the children decorate their animal and attach dowel handles to the back with sticky tape.
- Ask the children in which year their parents and grandparents were born and to find the animals representing these years.

50

16 Chinese dragon

Materials and preparation

· cardboard boxes · sticky tape
· scissors · paint · tissue paper · glue

 To use a range of materials to create a dragon. To dance

 To talk about differences in cultures

 To listen and respond to songs

New Year celebrations in China feature parades with dancing dragons.

EXTENSION IDEAS

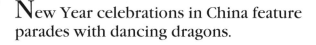

- Ask the children to stand up in the boxes and, while 'wearing' the dragon, process around the setting.
- Teach the children dragon songs such as 'Puff the Magic Dragon' by Peter Yarrow. Ask them to 'dance' the dragon.
- Talk about the difference between the scary dragon of English tradition and the Chinese dragon that brings good fortune.

▶ WHAT TO DO

- Help the children make their own Chinese dragon out of old boxes.
- Decorate cardboard boxes for the dragon's head and body. Cut holes in the front side of each box so the children can see out. Join the boxes together with sticky tape. Make a cardboard tail and draw on two nostrils.

👍 Use coloured crêpe paper to make flames for the dragon's nostrils.

17 Catching the dragon's tail

 To follow instructions. To play with other children

 To show a growing awareness of space. To move with confidence and increasing control

👍 Make sure you have plenty of space in which to play this game. It would be best to play outside on a safe surface.

To end your Chinese New Year celebrations, teach the children how to play this fun game.

▶ WHAT TO DO

- Choose one child as the head of the dragon. Ask the others to line up behind and to place their hands on the shoulders of the child in front. The last person in the line is the tail. Give a signal and ask the head to run around trying to catch the tail. If the body of the 'dragon' breaks then the head moves to the tail and the next person in the line becomes the head. If the head catches the tail then the head remains
- Give all the children a chance to be the head.

👍 Encourage skill and co-ordination rather than speed.

CYCLOPEDIA OF CELEBRATIONS

This chapter gives background information for adults on all of the festivals and celebrations featured in this book. It is not meant as reading material for children. The basis for each celebration is explained, as are different ways of celebrating them, helping to inspire you to extend the activities in your setting.

Spring

Japanese Doll Festival

Hina Matsuri, which translates as 'Festival of the Dolls', falls on March 3 and is a traditional Japanese festival that promotes the love of children, especially girls. Peach blossom, prevalent in Japan at this time of year, is used to represent gentility, composure and tranquillity and is seen as a symbol of happy marriage. The festival finds its origin in a Japanese tradition where families used to place straw dolls next to babies to ward off illness and bad luck. The dolls were then either offered up to shrines or put on wooden boats and cast out to sea or down a river to carry the bad luck away; these traditions continue today. Girls in the family, nowadays, have a special collection of ornamental dolls; these are too precious to play with normally and are only brought out to honour the festival. Often a family will have a designated room where a set of tiered steps are arranged and covered with a red sheet. The children then display their dolls on the steps. The emperor and empress dolls take pride of place on the top tier of the display. On the next level down there are, traditionally, two lords, three court ladies, five musicians and three servants. Food and furniture are often displayed on the lower levels. Activities relating to this celebration appear on page 19.

Carnival

The word 'carnival' comes from the Latin 'carne vale' which means 'without meat'. It is believed that carnival celebrations can be traced back to a pagan festival in ancient Rome or Greece. Across the world it is the festival that precedes the fasting of Lent, that is the forty day period before Easter when some Christian families still avoid meat to commemorate Jesus' time in the wilderness. In Rio de Janeiro, Brazil, the carnival lasts four days and culminates in 'Mardi Gras' (literally 'Fat Tuesday') the day before Lent begins. The event is a joyous occasion full of music and colour. For many, the highlight of the festival is the parade of floats and Samba dancers that process through the city, a tradition that started in the 1930s. Samba troupes choose a special theme to represent through dance in the parade, and spend weeks practising their routines. On the day, they dress up in bright, glittery costumes and wear feathers and beads in their hair. Similarly, groups will spend months choosing

a theme and building their floats in preparation for the biggest party of the year. People gather in a square and then follow the procession down a pre-determined route to the music of bands and orchestras. Activities relating to this celebration appear on pages 20–21.

Easter

The Christian festival of Easter falls on the first Sunday after the first full moon following the spring equinox (which itself falls on March 21). The word 'Easter' is thought to have derived from the name of the Saxon goddess of spring, Eostre. This happy festival is preceded by the 40-day fast of Lent, observed by Christians in remembrance of Jesus' fasting and repentance in the wilderness. The Friday before Easter Sunday, called Good Friday, solemnly commemorates the death of Jesus Christ, the son of the Christian God. Church services centre on the story leading up to the death of Jesus, commonly called the Passion. Easter, however, is a joyous occasion, celebrating Jesus' triumph over death and resurrection to life. It is one of the most important events in the Christian calendar and is celebrated across the world; for instance the Pope, the head of the Roman Catholic Church, traditionally holds a service in Rome, Italy, in front of crowds of tens of thousands of worshippers and prays for people in many different languages. Christian believers dress smartly and go to church on Easter Sunday morning to hear how Jesus rose from the dead and to give thanks to God for delivering them from evil. In many countries, the egg is a popular image of Easter as it signifies the appearance of new life; Christian doctrine teaches that, by sacrificing Himself, Jesus gave all Christians the chance to enjoy life after death with God in heaven. In some countries, especially in Europe and the United States, families organise egg-hunting games. Chocolate eggs are hidden around the garden and the young children of the family are allowed to go out to try to find as many as possible. Activities relating to this celebration appear on pages 22–23.

Holi

Holi is a Hindu festival that falls in late February or early March and is a celebration of the gathering of the wheat and mustard harvest. Holi finds its origin deep in Indian tradition. Legend states that the ancient King, Hiranyakashup, ordered all to worship him as a god. When his son, Prahlad, refused, the King tried many ways to kill him but was continually thwarted. Finally, the King asked his own sister, Holika (after whom the festival was named) who was reportedly unable to be harmed by flames, to lead Prahlad to his death into a blazing fire; Holika, however, burned to death and Prahlad survived by the will of the Hindu God. The night before Holi, fires are lit, both to signify spiritual enlightenment in people's hearts and to ward off evil spirits. As the fire rages, a burning branch is removed to symbolise the saving of Prahlad. Some people even cook pine nuts in the fire. Holi is sometimes called 'The Festival of Colour' owing to a tradition that stems from Krishna, the human form of the Hindu God, Vishnu. Krishna used to play around in the water with his female companion, Radha, splashing and squirting her with water. In modern-day India, people remember Krishna by mixing water with coloured powder paints and squirting the mixture all over others. This is seen as a fun way of making friends and breaking down the usual cultural barriers that exist in Indian society. Activities relating to this celebration appear on page 24.

Eid-ul-Fitr

Eid starts when the new moon is sighted at the end of Ramadan, the ninth month of the Islamic calendar. Ramadan is the month of fasting and is one of the five Pillars of Islam. These are five elements that Muslims must adhere to throughout their lives, the others being belief in their God Allah, prayers five times each day, pilgrimage to the holy city of Mecca once in their lifetime and charity. As a Muslim, you are not allowed to eat or drink between sunrise and sunset throughout the month of Ramadan. This is meant to give Muslims time for introspection and the chance to thank Allah for his blessings over the year. It is also a good time to remember people in need; many people donate alms to the poor. Eid-ul-Fitr, which means 'breaking of the fast', is a time to celebrate the end of Ramadan. On the morning of Eid, Muslims dress in their best clothes, new if they can afford it, and go to the mosque to say prayers. A special sermon is given, then the congregation rise and hug each other, saying 'Eid Mubarak', which means 'Holiday Blessings'. After prayers, people often go to visit friends or relatives where they enjoy an Eid day meal and exchange money and other gifts. Eid celebrations can last up to three days. Activities relating to this celebration appear on page 25.

Summer

Çocuk Bayrami

In 1920 Mustafa Kemal Atatürk declared 23 April as Turkish Children's Day, or Çocuk Bayrami. Mustafa Kemal was a much-loved leader of the Turks and the acknowledged founder of the modern state of Turkey. Such was the people's love for Kemal, that he became known as 'Atatürk', which literally means 'father of the Turks'. Atatürk was well known for his love of children; during his 15-year rule as leader of Turkey, he 'adopted' a number of youngsters and paid for their schooling and upkeep until he died in 1938. Atatürk realised the importance of children in society and so introduced this festival, both to instil a sense of national pride in the children and to highlight their important position in the community. In more recent times, Çocuk Bayrami has become the focus for an international children's event, with youngsters coming from all over the world to celebrate in Ankara, Turkey's capital city. Turkish children dress up for the occasion, wearing either fancy dress or national costumes particular to regions of the country. Traditional items of clothing include long gowns called kaftans, baggy trousers called salvar and brightly coloured sashes worn around the waist. Children across the country hold ceremonies and parades and stage plays and special dances in honour of their former leader. During the celebrations, children from the Turkish Scouts help to plant young trees to remind both children and adults of the importance of environmental issues. Street sellers offer a range of traditional Turkish snacks, such as köfte, which are grilled meatballs served in pitta bread, and burma which are sticky sweets made with pistachio nuts and honey. Activities relating to this celebration appear on page 27.

World Environment Day

World Environment Day is an annual event that falls on June 5. Unlike many of the festivals in this book, it is an international event not bound by culture or religion. The occasion was first initiated by the United Nations General Assembly during the Stockholm Conference on the Human Environment in 1972. The aim of World Environment Day is to highlight the ever-growing problems faced by our planet and to underline that community action is pivotal in addressing these problems. The organisers hope to achieve a number of objectives. First and foremost they want to show members of the public what they can do to help preserve the planet and how best to do it. Secondly, they hope to highlight that humans and the environment are interdependent, relying on each other to be able to survive. Finally, the organisers aim to promote sufficiency and moderation, as opposed to the greed and excess that characterises much of the world today. The event is based in a different major city each year, although activities are organised all over the world. It was last held in the United Kingdom in 1994. Television stations run documentaries highlighting various environmental issues and there are plenty of opportunities to attend art exhibitions, seminars and meetings. Every year is underpinned by a different theme, such as the ozone layer and global warming, and this becomes the main priority to concentrate on for that year. The theme in 1990, for example, was 'Children and the Environment'. Members of the public organise rallies and bicycle parades to promote the event and in many countries 'green' concerts are staged to help raise money. Some even hold mass recycling or tree-planting events. During each World Environment Day, awards are handed out to people who have made valuable contributions to environmental issues. Activities relating to this celebration appear on pages 28-29.

Midsummer Day

Falling on June 24, Midsummer Day shares its day of celebration with St John the Baptist, the Christian martyr. In medieval Britain, tradition stated that all spring work in the fields should be finished by Midsummer Day. Families would then clean their homes from top to bottom and decorate their rooms with branches from St John's Day trees, which we know as birch trees. Families in Britain, and in other countries such as Spain, would light huge bonfires to ward off evil spirits, bad luck and illness.

It was believed that the dew that fell on Midsummer's night had curative properties; people used to roll around on the grass to protect themselves from illness for the following year. Evidence of celebration on Midsummer Day in Britain dates back many thousands of years, well before medieval tradition took hold. The site at Stonehenge, on Salisbury Plain in England, dates back over 4,000 years and is believed to have been a ceremonial meeting place for druids, Celtic priests, for whom Midsummer Day and the summer solstice were very important events. In Estonia, Midsummer Day celebrations come second only to Christmas in terms of importance. For Estonians it serves as a break between the sowing, happening during spring, and the hay making of summer. Estonians light fires on Midsummer Day and jump over them to invite prosperity for the coming year. Activities relating to this celebration appear on page 30.

Canada Day

Originally known as Dominion Day, Canada Day takes place on July 1 every year, unless it falls on a Sunday, in which case it is celebrated on July 2. The festival was brought in to commemorate the founding of the Canadian Federal Government following the British North American Act of 1867. Previously, Canada had existed only as a collection of different provinces under British rule, but was granted independence following Sir John A. MacDonald's negotiations in London. He returned as Canada's first Prime Minister and set about putting together a government made up of representatives from all over the country. The name 'Canada Day' was first adopted in 1982 following an act of parliament designed to play down the country's colonial origins. July 1 is a designated national holiday and the Canadian people celebrate by holding barbecues and attending firework displays, processions and fanfares put on in towns all over the country. In Toronto, one of Canada's largest cities, many of the celebrations centre around the harbour. A fleet of boats, each representing a different charity and decorated with lights and flags, sails through the harbour at night while thousands look on. These celebrations are based on a different theme each year; in 1999 the theme was 'Through the Eyes of a Child'. Activities relating to this celebration appear on page 31.

Independence Day

On July 4 every year, American citizens celebrate winning their independence in 1776 from British colonial rule. The end of the war with the British led to the drawing up of the Declaration of Independence by a group of men led by

Thomas Jefferson. Liberty Bell in Philadelphia was rung to announce the first public reading of the Declaration by Colonel John Nixon on July 8 1776. Every year on Independence Day, Liberty Bell is rung again to remind Americans of this important event in the history of their country. Bells in towns across America also toll to commemorate the founding of the nation; this is the most important secular event in the American calendar. Soon after the Declaration of Independence, the American people were presented with their new flag. The first design featured 13 stars and 13 stripes to represent the original colonies founded in America; the 13 stripes remain today but the flag now sports 52 stars, one for each of the American states. The star is seen as a symbol of dominion and sovereignty and the flag itself is seen to represent national independence. On the first anniversary of the signing of the Declaration in 1777, the people of Philadelphia broke into spontaneous celebration. It is now a national holiday and Americans hold barbecues and picnics and take the opportunity to visit members of their family. Firework displays take place all over the country and many towns organise parades with marching bands and floats. Some people precede the festivities by reading the Declaration and reflecting on its ideals. Whatever way people choose to celebrate, Independence Day is a joyous occasion. Activities relating to this celebration appear on page 32.

St Swithin's Day

English myth states that if it rains on St Swithin's Day, July 15, then it will rain every day for the next 40 days. St Swithin was chaplain to Egbert, King of the West Saxons and one of his most trusted counsellors. Swithin was entrusted with the schooling of Egbert's son Ethelwulf. In 852, after Ethelwulf had acceded to the throne, Swithin was appointed Bishop of Winchester. He reportedly was responsible for the building of several churches and was well known for his humility and work helping the poor and needy. St Swithin asked if, when he died, he could be buried outside the north wall of Winchester Cathedral to ensure the raindrops falling from the eaves would land on where he lay. Records show that, some time during the tenth century, St Swithin's body was exhumed and buried inside the Cathedral. Legend holds that there followed a great drought that lasted until the body was taken back out of the Cathedral and reburied according to St Swithin's original request. Activities relating to this celebration appear on page 33.

Autumn

Chinese kite festival

Falling some time between September 1 and 9, this festival is sometimes called 'Climbing the Heights'. According to legend, there was a clairvoyant, living during the Han dynasty in ancient China, who warned of an impending devastating natural disaster. Nobody heeded his warning, except for a man called Woon Ging. He took his family up to the top of a tall hill. Once on top of the hill, Woon Ging flew a kite to try to reach closer to heaven. The foretold disaster came and everybody was wiped out apart from Woon Ging and his family. Since then, people have believed that flying a kite would bring good luck and fortune. During the Qing dynasty (1644–1911), people used to fly kites and then let them go in the wind to release bad luck and illness. It was said that if someone then picked up the kite, the bad luck would be transferred to that person. Kites have always played a large part in Chinese culture, with records of their existence going back over 2,000 years. Kites are seen as the earliest forms of aircraft; ancient Chinese soldiers used to tie men to huge kites and fly them over battle fields to look at enemy positions and report back to their superiors. During the festival, people across the country fly thousands of different designs of kite; dragon kites are very popular as dragons are seen to represent life and creativity. Many of the kites have bells attached to them so they jangle in the wind, and at night some people attach small lanterns so they shine in the dark. In Weifang, China, widely accepted as the world kite capital, they hold a festival every year in April with singing, dancing, folk performances and competitions for the best, smallest and biggest kites. Activities relating to this celebration appear on page 35.

Harvest festival

Harvest festival in England falls on the same day as Michaelmas, the feast of St Michael, on September 29. Traditionally a joyous occasion, celebrating the gathering of corn, this festival is characterised by much feasting and merriment. The custom of celebrating the harvest can be traced back to pagan times when people used to worship the corn goddess Ceres. When collecting the wheat after the harvest, farmers used to believe that the last sheaf left in the field represented Ceres. They used to mould the sheaf into human form and then hang it in the local church or at home to bring luck to the next harvest. Nowadays, at harvest time, people often display miniature versions of the sheaf, called corn dollies. Another legend in England, in the county of Lincolnshire, holds that years ago an ugly creature appeared and tried to claim a farmer's land as its own. They eventually struck a bargain whereby the farmer would keep the bottom half of the crop and the creature would take the top. The farmer planted potatoes, keeping the crop himself and giving the worthless stalks to the creature. The creature eventually disappeared but now, if tools ever go missing around harvest time, Lincolnshire farmers blame it on the evil creature. Harvest in America is often linked to their festival of Thanksgiving. Americans give thanks to the Christian God for giving them food after the harsh winter suffered by the Pilgrim Fathers when they first arrived in Massachusetts. The native Americans helped the pilgrims

and showed them how to harvest the land, so the modern-day festival of Thanksgiving celebrates the bringing of people together. American families traditionally eat turkey, pumpkins and sweetcorn. Activities relating to this celebration appear on pages 36-37.

Halloween

Celebrated on October 31, Halloween dates back thousands of years and its origins can be found amongst the traditions of the Celts in Britain and northern Europe. They used to celebrate New Year on November 1, the end of the season of the sun, in preparation for the season of cold and darkness. According to legend, the sun god, whom Celts used to worship, was taken prisoner by Samhain, 'Lord of the dead and Prince of darkness', during the winter months. On the day before their New year, that is on October 31, Celts believed that Samhain gathered all the dead together who then took on the forms of animals and roamed the country causing trouble. Cats were seen as the most evil of the creatures. Druids, Celtic priests, would light fires in the woods amongst oak trees, which they believed to be sacred, and dance around and offer

sacrifices to ward off the evil spirits. They would then take embers from the fire and use them to light fires in their homes to keep them warm and free from evil during the winter months. When the Romans invaded Britain in 43 BC the Celtic festival became entwined with the Roman worship of Pamona. She was the goddess of fruits and gardens and it is from here that the association with apples and nuts that people eat at Halloween originates. The arrival of Christianity in Britain added new influences to the celebration. Christians celebrate All Saints Day on November 1. This feast day was originally called All Hallows Day. October 31 became known as All Hallows Eve, which later changed to Halloween. During the Christian festival, people used to dress up as angels, saints and devils. Nowadays, Halloween is celebrated in many countries across the world. Activities include apple bobbing, dressing up, making jack o' lanterns out of pumpkins to ward off evil, and trick-or-treating. In New York village, America, they have a Halloween parade every year where some 25,000 people dress up in costumes and march through the streets whilst bands play music. It is very much a fun event for all the family to enjoy. Activities relating to this celebration appear on page 38.

Guy Fawkes

On November 5 every year people across Britain celebrate Guy Fawkes' night. The celebration commemorates the Gunpowder Plot. In 1605, a man called Guy Fawkes and a group of co-conspirators tried to blow up The Houses of Parliament in London and kill the King, James 1. He was deporting Jesuit Catholics and the conspirators were not happy as they wanted Catholicism restored to England. One of the conspirators had a friend in Parliament and sent him an anonymous letter warning of the murder plot. The letter found its way to the King and the conspirators were arrested trying to plant 36 barrels of gunpowder underneath the Houses of Parliament. Some people believe that James 1 was aware of the plot all along as all those involved were well-known dissenters; it is thought they may have been set up to give the King an excuse to have them executed. It is unlikely that the conspirators would have been able to get hold of

and transport 36 barrels of gunpowder unnoticed. Children in Britain make an effigy, called a guy, using old clothes stuffed with newspaper or straw. The children sit on the street with their guy seeking donations to give to charity by asking the question 'penny for the guy?' On Guy Fawkes night, the effigy is mounted on top of a bonfire and burned. This tradition dates back to 1606 when people used to burn effigies of the Pope, the head of the Catholic church. It was not until 1806, however, that people started burning effigies of Guy Fawkes himself. In addition to the bonfire, families attend firework displays held all over the country to symbolise the attempted blowing up of Parliament. People then gather round the burning guy and eat food such as toffee apples and potatoes baked in the fire. Activities relating to this celebration appear on page 39.

Diwali

The Hindu festival of Diwali takes place during autumn, just before the new moon, when the sky is at its darkest. Amongst other things, it is a celebration of the abundance of the autumn harvest. After sunset on Diwali, Hindus pray to Lakshmi, the goddess of wealth and prosperity, as without the harvest there would be no prosperity for them to enjoy. The festival falls at the end of the rainy season, a period of the year when India is often afflicted by heavy flooding, which brings disease and bad smelling water into people's homes. Hindus encourage Lakshmi to

visit their homes by cleaning them thoroughly and whitewashing the walls. Thousands of years ago, in the north Indian province of Avadha, people celebrated the return of their benevolent Lord Rama from 14 years in exile following his defeat of the evil King Ravana. His people lit thousands of diva, small oil lamps in clay pots, to guide him home through the darkness. People still light diva today, although the mustard oil and wick originally used are sometimes replaced with small candles. Nowadays, diva help to light up the dark evenings so travellers can see their way and avoid potential dangers, such as snakes reappearing after sheltering from the rains. There is, therefore, a strong feeling of benevolence towards other people at Diwali. During the festival, people put on new clothes and attend the evening prayers offered to Lakshmi. Some people buy new clothes especially for Diwali. Children will touch their elders feet as a mark of respect and then share out food and sweets with friends and relatives. Fireworks, often bearing the image of Lakshmi, are available for sale on the streets all over India and are set off in the evening to ward off evil. Activities relating to this celebration appear on pages 40-41.

Winter

St Lucia day

The Swedish festival of Santa Lucia falls on December 13. St Lucia was a young Italian girl who lived in Sicily during the fourth century. This was a time when some of the earliest Christian persecutions were just beginning. Many Christians hid in underground tunnels. According to tradition, St Lucia, renowned for her kindness and love, used to bring food and provisions to those hiding from the authorities; she used to wear candles around her head so that she could find her way in the dark. Lucia took a vow of celibacy and so, when propositioned by a potential suitor, she turned him down. In his rage the suitor informed the authorities of the illegal aid she was giving to the fugitive Christians. She was sentenced to death by burning, but she prayed to God for his protection and was saved. Legend states that, when she was eventually killed by the sword, she spent her dying moments uttering words of comfort and love. Swedish schools, which usually close at noon on the day of the festival, select a different Lucia girl each year. She dresses up in a white tunic with a red sash tied around her waist and wears a crown of evergreen leaves, adorned with seven candles. The Lucia girl leads a procession, followed by maids dressed in white and boys wearing conical hats decorated with stars, all singing a well-known Lucia song. Often the procession will lead children to public places, such as town halls, where coffee is served with saffron-flavoured biscuits, called lussekattes. Activities relating to this celebration appear on page 43

Hanukkah

The Jewish festival of Hannukah begins on the 25th Day of the Jewish month of Kislev; usually December,

according to the Gregorian calendar. The history of this festival dates back to 167 BC when the Greeks, led by King Antiochus Epiphanes, ruled over the Jewish land of Israel. Epiphanes banned such Jewish rituals as keeping the Sabbath and ordered that Jews must sacrifice pigs to the

Greek gods. An old Jewish priest, Matthathias, saw a Jew about to offer a pig as a sacrifice and killed him, and then fled to the hills with his sons. From here he started a guerrilla movement with the aim of driving the Greeks from Israel. When he died his son, Judah the Maccabee, took over and led his army of Maccabeans to defeat all of Epiphanes' armies. When the Jews liberated Jerusalem, they found that the Greeks had defiled the temple, leaving only enough oil to keep the sacred lamp burning for one day. Although the journey to find more oil took eight days, the Jewish God performed a miracle and kept the lamp burning until the messenger returned. Every year Jews remember this miracle by lighting a new candle on each day of the festival of Hannukah. The candles are kept in a hannukiyah, a nine-branched holder; the extra candle, the shamash, is used to light the others. Hannukah is a family occasion where relatives get together to give thanks to God. Family meals consist of plenty of food fried in oil, such as latkes, to commemorate the miracle of the oil in the temple. People read the Torah, the Jewish Bible, sing traditional songs and exchange cards and gifts. Activities relating to this celebration appear on pages 44-45.

Christmas

All over the world on December 25, Christian families

celebrate the birth of Jesus. This festival is called Christmas. The origins of this festival and many of the modern-day Christmas traditions, can be traced back thousands of years. In Mesopotamia, for example, the 12-day festival of Zagmuk celebrated the arrival of the new year. Here, the King had to swear faith to the God Marduk and then sacrifice his life to fight at Marduk's side. To spare their King, however, Mesopotamians used to slay a common criminal in his place. In northern Scandinavia, where winter heralds weeks of darkness, messengers used to stand on top of a hill to look out for the first signs of light. People used to celebrate round a huge fire, burning a Yule log, when the first light came; this festival became known as Yuletide. Similarly, during December the Romans enjoyed the festival of Saturnalia where they used to have huge meals and give gifts to one another to celebrate the beginning of the end of the dark months of winter. As

Christianity spread, this pagan festival was adopted to celebrate the birth of Jesus Christ, the 'light of the world'. The festival was fixed on December 25 by Pope Liberius in 354 AD. During Christmas, Christians remember the story leading up to Jesus' birth, giving gifts to commemorate the gifts given to Jesus by the Three Wise Men. The history of the Christmas tree dates back to the seventh century. St Boniface, while touring England, teaching the word of God, used the triangular shape of the fir tree to help explain the trinity of the Father, Son and Holy Spirit. It was not until the 16th century, however, when Martin Luther put candles on a fir tree to describe a starlit walk he had taken in a forest, that people began to adorn their trees with lights. Nowadays, trees form the centrepiece for Christmas decorations in homes all over the world. In England, families gather for a big Christmas meal and traditionally eat turkey and exchange gifts. Mexican children enjoy a tradition where they repeatedly hit a clay pot suspended from the ceiling until it breaks, covering them with toys or sweets. Activities relating to this celebration appear on pages 46-48.

New Year

Celebrations for New Year, which falls on January 1, start the night before, on December 31. The start of a new year was first celebrated in Babylon some 4,000 years ago. The Babylonian year began on March 23 as this date signalled the beginning of spring and the planting of new crops. It was the Roman senate who decreed, in 153 BC, that the year would begin on January 1, having previously celebrated it on March 25. New Year celebrations were originally seen as pagan by the Christian church but they soon became intertwined with their own festival of Christmas, which celebrated the birth of Christ. It has, however, only been recognised as a holiday in the West for the last 400 years. In Scotland, a country renowned for its New Year celebrations, the overriding theme is that of beginning the new year on a happy note. Activities relating to this celebration appear on page 49.

Kwanzaa

The Afro-American festival of Kwanzaa begins on December 26 and lasts until January 1. It was established in 1966 by Dr Maulana Karenga, a professor in the Department of Black Studies at California State University. Brought in during the Black Liberation movement of the 1960s, Kwanzaa calls on black people to remember and reaffirm their African culture and traditions. It takes its name from the Swahili 'matunda ya kwanza', which means 'first fruits', a reference to the African harvest festival on which Kwanzaa is based. The celebrations underline seven principles to follow: unity, self-determination, collective work and responsibility, co-operative economics, purpose, creativity and faith. On the final night of Kwanzaa a feast is held called Karamu. House decorations are dominated by the Kwanza setting; a display on a straw mat that includes crops, gifts, a candle holder, candles, one ear of corn for each child in the family and one unity cup. The Kinara, the candle holder, holds seven candles, one black, three red and three green. Black represents the people, red their struggle and green their hope and future. These three colours are prevalent in most Kwanzaa decorations. At the feast everyone drinks from the cup of unity, remembers the past and commits themselves to a prosperous future. Any gifts that are exchanged must include a book and a symbol of African heritage to underline the importance of learning and tradition. Activities relating to this celebration appear on pages 48-49.

Chinese New Year

The Chinese New Year celebrations last for 15 days. The date for the beginning of the new year moves every year, as the Chinese calendar relies on a combination of the lunar and solar cycles. Nowadays, Chinese New Year is commonly known as The Spring Festival. The Chinese word for 'year' is 'nian', the name of a monster who used to come out and prey on people on the eve of the new year. The people used to paint red designs (the monster was terrified of the colour red) onto their houses and set off firecrackers to scare the monster away. One day an old man appeared, tricked the monster into eating all the other dangerous beasts and then rode it away from the people who were then left to live in peace. It transpired that the old man was an immortal God. People now clean their houses to rid them of bad luck and decorate them with paper cut-outs to usher in prosperity and happiness for the coming year. Families gather on the eve of the new year to share a meal and play games. Throughout the course of that night all lights are left on in the houses and the skies are lit with fireworks and firecrackers. The following morning children are given gifts of money wrapped in red paper. The Chinese New Year festivities end with the Lantern festival, where young men perform

dances under an ornamental dragon whilst other people follow the processions carrying a range of different lamps. Activities relating to this celebration appear on pages 50-51.

Resources

This section contains suggestions for a useful range of material to supplement the activities in this book. The book list below contains a selection of fiction books that include stories, poems, rhymes, and songs as well as some suggestions for non-fiction information books. You will find templates to support The Chinese New Year activity on pages 62-63. The index on page 64 lists every activity contained in **All About Celebration**.

STORY BOOKS

'A Dark, Dark Tale', Ruth Brown. Red Fox

'A Letter to Father Christmas', Rose Impey and Sue Porter. Orchard Books

'After the Storm', Nick Butterworth. Collins

'Ben's Birthday Party', Rosemary Border. MacDonald

'The Berenstain Bears and the Spooky Old Tree', Stan and Jan Berenstain. Collins

'Cinderella', retold by Stan Cullimore. Pelican Big Books

'The Dragon of an Ordinary Family', Helen Oxenbury and Margaret Mahy. Mammoth

'Dear Greenpeace', Simon James. Walker Books

'Each Peach Pear Plum', Janet and Allan Ahlberg. Picture Puffin

'Easter', Jan Pienkowski. Mammoth

'Farmer Barnes' Guy Fawkes Day', J Cunliffe. André Deutsche

'Follow Jo's Kite', Belinda Evans. Piccadilly Press

'Having a Picnic', Sarah Garland. Puffin Books

'I Feel Angry', Brian Moses and Mike Gordon. Wayland.

'I Feel Sad', Brian Moses and Mike Gordon. Wayland

'It's My Birthday', Helen Oxenbury. Walker Books

'Jasper's Beanstalk', Nick Butterworth and Mick Inkpen. Hodder and Stoughton

'Jesus' Christmas Party', Nicholas Allan. Red Fox

'The Jolly Christmas Postman', Janet and Allan Ahlberg. Heinemann

'The Jolly Postman', Janet and Allan Ahlberg. Heinemann

'Kipper's Book of Weather', Mick Inkpen. Hodder

'The Last Dragon', Susan Miho Nunes. Houghton Mifflin

'Little Chick's Easter Surprise', Lois Rock. Lion

'The Little Red Hen', Gerald Rose. Cambridge University Press

'Meg and Mog' series, Helen Nicholl and Jan Pienkowski. Puffin

'Monkey in the Stars', Jamila Gavin. Mammoth

'Nina at Carnival', Errol Lloyd. Bodley Head

'One Smiling Grandma', Anne Marie Linden. Mammoth

'The Patchwork Quilt', Valerie Flournoy and Jerry Pinkney. Puffin

'The Picnic', Ruth Brown. Red Fox

'Rama and the Demon King', Jessica Souhami. Frances Lincoln

'Teddy Bear's Picnic', Mark Burgess. Picture Lions

'The Tiny Seed', Eric Carle. Puffin

'Up and Up', Shirley Hughes. Red Fox

'The Upstairs Downstairs Bears at Christmas', Carol Lawson. Mammoth

'What Will the Weather Be Like Today?', Paul Kazuko Roagers. Orchard Books

'Winnie the Witch' series, Valerie Thomas. Oxford University Press

Resources

INFORMATION BOOKS

'A Calendar of Festivals' (including a section on Kwanzaa), Cherry Gilchrist and Helen Cann. Barefoot Books

'All Saints, All Souls and Halloween', 'Chinese New Year', 'Christmas', 'Holi', 'Ramadam and Id-ul Fitr' (A World of Festivals Series). Evans

'A Seed in Need – A First Look at the Plant Cycle'. MacDonald Young Books

'All Ways of Looking at Seeds, Bulbs and Spores', J Walker. Franklin Watts

'Birdfeeder Handbook', Robert Burton. Dorling Kindersley

'Birds' Spotter's Guide series, Philip Holden. Usborne.

'The Book of Kites', Paul and Helene Morgan. Dorling Kindersley

'Catch the Wind', G Gibbons. Little Brown

'Celebration!', B. and A. Kindersley. Dorling Kindersley

'Chinese New Year', Sarah Moise. Wayland

'Dragons and Demons', S. Ross. Franklin Watts

'Easter Fun Book', Lois Rock. Lion

'Eyewitness – Flag', Dorling Kindersley

'Famous People, Famous Lives – Guy Fawkes', Harriet Caster. Franklin Watts

'Festivals of the Christian Year' Celebrate series, Lois Rock. Lion

'Festivals Together', Sue Fitzjohn, Minda Weston and Judy Large. Hawthorn Press

'Festivals', Jean Gilbert. Oxford University Press

'Fiesta – Turkey', Tessa Paul. Franklin Watts

'Find Out About the Weather', Terry Jennings. BBC Books

'The Great Games Book', Susan Adams. Dorling Kindersley

'Guy Fawkes', Clare Chandler. Wayland

'Harvest', Clare Chandler. Wayland

'Hindu Temples' Places of Worship series, Margaret Griffin. Heinemann

'Judaism', Sue Penney. Heinemann

'Kwanzaa and Me', Vivian Paley. Harvard University Press

'Let's Discover Churches', C Bradley. Franklin Watts

'Managing Your Curriculum', Ruth Andreski and Sarah Nicholls. Times Supplements

'The Moon' Windows on the Universe series, Robert Estalella. Belitha

'My First Cook Book', Angela Wilkes. Dorling Kindersley

'My First Green Book', Angela Wilkes. Dorling Kindersley

'My Hindu Life', Dilip Kadodwala and Sharon Chhapi. Wayland

'My Jewish Life', Anne Clark and David Rose. Wayland

'My Muslim Life', Riadh El Droubie. Wayland

'Religious Articles', Anita Ganeri. Wayland

'Religious Buildings', Anita Ganeri. Wayland

'Santa's Sackful of Best Christmas Ideas', D Robins. Kingfisher

'Space' Windows on the World series, S Becklake. Dorling Kindersley

'Spring Festivals', 'Summer Festivals', 'Autumn Festivals', 'Winter Festivals', Mike Rosen. Wayland

'Sultan's Kitchen – Turkish Cookbook', Ozcan Ozan. Periplus Editions

'The Usborne Children's Bible'. Usborne

'The Usborne Flags Sticker Book'. Usborne

'The Visual Dictionary of Plants'. Dorling Kindersley

'The World of Festivals', Phillip Steele. McDonald Young Books

'This Little Puffin', ed. Elizabeth Matterson. Puffin

'What Do We Know About Islam?', Shahrukh Hussain. MacDonald Young Books

'Where Food Comes From', J Cook. Usborne

Festivals of the World series, Heinemann

SONGS, POEMS, RHYMES AND MUSIC

'Big Book of Rhymes and Stories', Chosen by Ronne Randall. Ladybird

'Earthways, Earthwise – Poems on Conservation', selected by Judith Nicholls. Oxford University Press

'Harlequin – 44 Songs Round the Year', A & C Black

'One Little Candle' can be found in 'A Musical Calendar of Festivals', Chosen by Barbara Cass-Beggs. Ward Lock Educational

'Puff the Magic Dragon', Peter Yarrow can be found in 'Tinderbox – 66 Songs for Children', A & C Black

'Turkey – Bektashi Music', Unesco Collection. Auvidis

Templates

Chinese New Year masks templates for The Year of the... (15) page 50

Rat: 1936, 1948, 1960, 1972, 1984, 1996, 2008

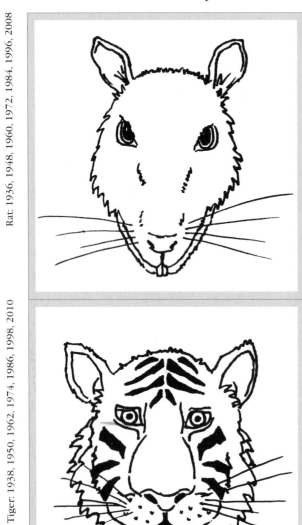

Ox: 1937, 1949, 1961, 1973, 1985, 1997, 2009

Tiger: 1938, 1950, 1962, 1974, 1986, 1998, 2010

Hare: 1939, 1951, 1963, 1975, 1987, 1999, 2011

Dragon: 1940, 1952, 1964, 1976, 1988, 2000, 2012

Snake: 1941, 1953, 1965, 1977, 1989, 2001, 2013

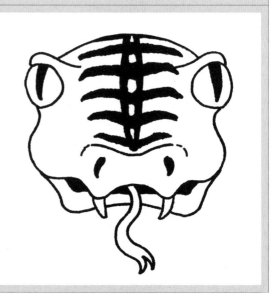

Chinese New Year masks

Horse: 1930, 1942, 1954, 1966, 1978, 1990, 2002

Ram: 1931, 1943, 1955, 1967, 1979, 1991, 2003

Monkey: 1932, 1944, 1956, 1968, 1980, 1992, 2004

Cockerel: 1933, 1945, 1957, 1969, 1981, 1993, 2005

Dog: 1934, 1946, 1958, 1970, 1982, 1994, 2006

Pig: 1935, 1947, 1959, 1971, 1983, 1995, 2007

Index

Acknowledgments

Nursery World would like to thank:

Hope Education for providing many of the props used in this book; Jim Copley for props and templates; Neil Thompson for digital music; Turtle and Pearce for the flags on page 31; Creative Quilting for the patchwork quilt on page 48; Denise Blake for picture research; Stephen Harper for the photograph bottom left of page 22; Agency picture credits: Roderick Johnson/Images of India, for the photograph top of page 24; Peter Sanders, for the photograph top of page 41.